Globalization of Capital and the Nation-State

Globalization of Capital and the Nation-State

Imperialism, Class Struggle, and the State in the Age of Global Capitalism

Berch Berberoglu

ROWMAN & LITTLEFIELD PUBLISHERS, INC.
Lanham • Boulder • New York • Oxford

ROWMAN & LITTLEFIELD PUBLISHERS, INC.

Published in the United States of America
by Rowman & Littlefield Publishers, Inc.
A Member of the Rowman & Littlefield Publishing Group
4501 Forbes Boulevard, Suite 200, Lanham, Maryland 20706
www.rowmanlittlefield.com

P.O. Box 317, Oxford OX2 9RU, United Kingdom

British Library Cataloguing in Publication Information Available

Library of Congress Cataloging-in-Publication Data

Berberoglu, Berch.
  Globalization of capital and the nation-state : imperialism, class
struggle, and the state in the age of global capitalism / Berch
Berberoglu.
     p. cm.
Includes bibliographical references and index.
  ISBN 0-7425-2494-9 (cloth : alk. paper) — ISBN 0-7425-2495-7 (pbk. :
alk. paper)
  1. Capitalism. 2. Globalization. 3. Imperialism. 4. International
business enterprises. 5. Competition, International. 6. State, The.
7. United States—Foreign economic relations. 8. Economic
history—1990- 9. Social history—1970- I. Title.
  HB501.B444 2003
  337—dc21

                                              2002155354

Printed in the United States of America

∞™ The paper used in this publication meets the minimum requirements of American
National Standard for Information Sciences—Permanence of Paper for Printed Library
Materials, ANSI/NISO Z39.48-1992.

Contents

Preface and Acknowledgments

The globalization of capital—the accumulation of capital from the national to the international level, where the worldwide operations of the transnational corporations have led to the rise of vast capitalist empires across the world—had developed long before the concept of "globalization" became fashionable among Western intellectuals during the closing decades of the twentieth and the turn of the twenty-first centuries.

Writing in the early twentieth century, John A. Hobson, a liberal British political economist and member of Parliament, was among the very first critics of British imperialism who in his book *Imperialism: A Study* ([1905] 1972) pointed out in no uncertain terms the very essence of the global expansion of capital and the domination of the global economy by capitalist interests that defined the nature and dynamics of international economic relations and, by extension, political relations of control and domination of the world by powerful financial interests. "Imperialism," wrote Hobson, "implies the use of the machinery of government by private interests, mainly capitalist, to secure for them economic gains outside their country" (94). He went on to state, "The economic root of Imperialism is the desire of strong organized industrial and financial interests to secure and develop at the public expense and by the public force private markets for their surplus goods and their surplus capital" (106). "The growing cosmopolitanism of capital," he added, "has been the greatest economic change of recent generations. Every advanced industrial nation has been tending to place a larger share of its capital outside the limits of its own political area, in foreign countries, in colonies, and to draw a growing income from this source" (51). Thus, "aggressive Imperialism . . . is a source of great gain to the investor who cannot find at home the profitable use he seeks for his capital and insists that his government should help him to profitable and secure investments abroad" (55).

Extending Hobson's analysis of British imperialism to the rest of the capitalist world and placing it in historical context and in class terms, Rosa Luxemburg in *The Accumulation of Capital* ([1913] 1951) and V. I. Lenin in *Imperialism: The Highest Stage of Capitalism* ([1917] 1975) developed a general Marxist theory of capitalist imperialism, viewing it as an extension of the logic of capital accumulation and capitalist development on a world scale.

I develop the arguments of these early theorists of imperialism at the beginning of this book, and apply these theories to explain the globalization of capital and its relation to the nation-state in the rest of the book. I argue that unlike what has been claimed by various authors in recent years, "globalization" is *not* a new phenomenon or a new stage of the world economy that represents a qualitatively different form of socioeconomic, political, and cultural relations designed to promote development and social progress around the world. I argue that globalization is now, under conditions of transnational monopoly capital, the highest and most accelerated stage of capitalist imperialism—that is, it is a global extension of transnational capital and the entire capitalist system that has penetrated every corner of the world and has done so with exceptional speed and intensity.

This book provides a comprehensive analysis of the nature, contradictions, and development of capitalist imperialism and the globalization process as its highest and most widespread expression throughout the world. Examining the dynamics of capital accumulation and its inherent (class) contradictions over the course of modern history, the various chapters contained in this book expose the inner workings of the capitalist system at the national and global levels. The role of the nation-state in this context of capitalist development is widely emphasized to explain the logic of the global political economy under the hegemony of the United States as the leading imperialist power in the late twentieth and early twenty-first centuries.

An undertaking of this scope, as I have done in this book, relies on many years of research, analysis, and reflection. Thus, many of the chapters included in this book have been brought together from scattered material published in several of my more than twenty authored and edited books written over the course of the past two decades. The consolidation of my writings on imperialism and globalization in a single book provides the reader with a comprehensive analysis of the dynamics of transnational capitalist expansion. Thus, this book makes an important contribution to an understanding of the dynamics and contradictions of imperialism and globalization, thereby generating a much needed discussion and debate on this critical issue of our time.

The topics discussed in this book were inspired by my teacher and mentor Albert Szymanski during my doctoral studies in sociology at the University of Oregon in the mid-1970s. The bulk of the work that I undertook during this period resulted in the publication of my book a decade later *The Internationalization of Capital: Imperialism and Capitalist Development on a World Scale* (1987b). This was followed by two other books: *Political Sociology: A Comparative/Historical Approach* (1990, 2001), which analyzes the nature and role of the state, and *The Political Economy of Development: Development Theory and the Prospects for Change in the Third World* (1992b), which investigates the dynamics of development under conditions of worldwide imperialist domination.

Throughout the 1990s, I published a number of additional books addressing these and related issues, ranging from *The Legacy of Empire: Economic Decline and Class Polarization in the United States* (1992a), which examines the rise and decline of the U.S. economy in the 1970s and 1980s, to *Labor and Capital in the Age of Globalization: The Labor Process and the Changing Nature of Work in the Global Economy* (2002), which scrutinizes the labor process and relations between labor and capital under conditions of globalization.

Most of the chapters in this book originally appeared in my earlier books published over the course of the past fifteen years. Chapters 1, 4, 5, 7, and parts of 8 are from *The Legacy of Empire* (1992a); chapters 3, 6, and parts of 8 were originally published in *The Political Economy of Development* (1992b); chapter 2 was published in *The Internationalization of Capital* (1987a); chapter 9 was originally entitled "Imperialism and Class Struggle in the Late 20th Century" and published in the journal *Humanity and Society* (1996). While my books *The Legacy of Empire* and *The Political Economy of Development* are currently out of print and their copyright has reverted back to me, I thank Nora Johnson, the rights and permissions coordinator at Praeger, for granting me permission to publish chapter 2 from another of my books, *The Internationalization of Capital* (1987b). I would also like to thank Corey Dolgon, editor of *Humanity and Society,* for granting me permission to publish chapter 9. My thanks go to all these publishers for enabling me to bring together my writings on imperialism and globalization in this book. The complete revision and updating of the original data and analysis provided in each chapter makes this book an especially important undertaking to spark debate on this important and controversial topic that will be discussed for years to come.

Friends and colleagues who have contributed to the shaping of my ideas on imperialism and globalization that are prominent in much of my writings over the past two decades include Albert Szymanski, James Petras, Blain Stevenson, Larry Reynolds, Walda Katz-Fishman, Alan Spector, Gianfranco Pala, Carla Filosa, David L. Harvey, Johnson Makoba, and David Lott. These and numerous other colleagues have had direct or indirect impact on the arguments presented in these pages, notwithstanding the fact that we have not always agreed on some of the points raised on the various topics that we have discussed and debated for a number of years.

The rapid development of world capitalism through the globalization of capital and the transformation of the state in recent decades makes the continuation of the debate on imperialism and globalization imperative, as the global expansion of capital and its contradictions will increasingly necessitate a clear understanding of its nature and dynamics and thus assist us in our efforts to critique and change it.

Globalization of Capital and the Nation-State

Introduction:
The Political Economy of Globalization and Its Contradictions

While waiting for my flight at New York's John F. Kennedy International Airport on my way to a conference on globalization in Cairo, Egypt, in early November 2000, I came across a copy of the latest issue of *Business Week* with the cover story "Special Report: Global Capitalism." In it, the report says, "It's hard to figure how a term that once meant so much good for the world has fallen into such disrepute. In the past decade, globalization—meaning the rise of market capitalism around the world—has undeniably contributed to America's [global economic] boom," while at the same time "multinationals have contributed to labor, environmental, and human-rights abuses." Mentioning that "workers toil 16 hours a day for miserly pay making garments sold in the U.S.," and citing World Bank data that "the number of people living on $1 a day has increased to 1.3 billion over the past decade," the *Business Week* report states, "The overwhelming conclusion of this reporting is that there are many examples of where reckless investment has done harm" so that "the downside of global capitalism is the disruption of whole societies. . . . [I]f global capitalism's flaws aren't addressed," continues the report, "the backlash could grow more severe" (Engardio 2000, 72, 74–75).

James Petras and Henry Veltmeyer in their book *Globalization Unmasked: Imperialism in the 21st Century* expose the reality behind globalization as the latest phase of global capitalist expansion that should be characterized as nothing less than the continuation of the operation of modern capitalist imperialism on a worldwide basis (2001, 12). In this context, the critical issue "is what the discourse on globalization is designed to hide and obfuscate: the form taken by imperialism in the current, increasingly worldwide capitalist system for organizing economic production and society" (13).

1

This book provides a critical analysis of the globalization process, high-lighting its dynamics and contradictions in the social, economic, and political spheres and its impact on the working class throughout the world in the late twentieth and early twenty-first centuries. I argue that the shift in production from the advanced capitalist centers to the peripheral areas of the world econ-omy has occurred as part of the accelerated globalization of capital and the international division of labor, facilitating the exploitation of labor through-out the world. Such exploitation, which is the basis of capital accumulation under global capitalism, leads to increased class conflict, class struggles, and ultimately to major social transformations.

Assessing the situation in broader political-economic terms, I argue that the contradictions embedded in the structure of contemporary global capitalism will lead to the intensification of class struggles around the world that are bound to develop in response to the accelerated globalization of capital in this latest phase of global capitalist expansion, especially since September 11, 2001.

THE NATURE AND DYNAMICS OF GLOBALIZATION

In a way of a definition, I would argue that globalization is the highest and most advanced stage of capitalist imperialism facilitated by transnational cap-ital for the intensification of capitalist expansion throughout the world. I argue that globalization

1. is an accelerated and much more pervasive phase of advanced monopoly capitalism operating on a worldwide scale than earlier stages of imperial-ism, and
2. is, in this sense, a continuation of transnational capitalist expansion throughout the world, defined by its new and more characteristic features (i.e., its speed and intensity) that are specific to this most current phase of global capitalist development.

A central feature of this current phase of transnational capitalism, besides its speed and intensity, is the increased privatization of various spheres of the economy and society with a proportionate decline in the power and ability of the state and other political institutions to control their national economies rel-ative to earlier periods (Rao 1998). Under the current wave of globalization, the state in the advanced capitalist societies (and increasingly in the less de-veloped ones) has lost not only some of its traditional power in controlling and regulating the various spheres of society, especially the economy, but also other areas such as communications, information technology, education, and the cultural sphere, where privatization is becoming increasingly prevalent. However, this does not mean that the state has lost its power completely, as it continues to be the chief administrator of power and holds on to its monopoly of force. Still, while the state persists in playing a prominent role in the public sphere, the current phase of global capitalist expansion has placed the transnational corporations in a more visible position where they have increasingly taken center stage in effecting changes in the global political economy, including some of the areas traditionally controlled by the state (Waters 1995; Halliday 2001).

The rate at which these changes have been taking place, and the vigor with which transnational capital has been exercising more power vis-à-vis the state, has led some to declare globalization a qualitatively new stage in the development of world capitalism (Ross and Trachte 1990). However, I argue that these quantitative, surface manifestations of contemporary capitalism, no matter how pervasive they are, do *not* change the fundamental nature of capitalism and capitalist relations, nor the nature of the capitalist/imperialist state and the class contradictions generated by these relations, which are inherent characteristics of the system itself. They cannot change the nature of capitalism in any qualitative sense to warrant globalization a distinct status that these critics have come to assign as something fundamentally different than what Marxist political economists have always argued to be the "normal" operation and evolution of global capitalism in the age of imperialism (Szymanski 1981; Warren 1980; Beams 1998; Foster 2002).

Globalization, then, much as during the earlier stages of capitalism, is driven by the logic of *profit* for the private accumulation of capital based on the exploitation of labor throughout the world. It is, in essence, the highest and most pervasive phase of transnational capitalism operating on a world scale. It is the most widespread and penetrating manifestation of modern capitalist imperialism in the age of the Internet—a development that signifies not only the most thorough economic domination of the world by the biggest capitalist monopolies, but also increasingly direct military intervention by the chief imperialist state to secure the global economic position of its own corporations, especially in controlling sources of raw materials (such as oil), as in the latest (March 2003) invasion of and war against Iraq by the United States and its junior coalition partner Britain.

GLOBALIZATION: ITS PARTICULAR CHARACTERISTICS

Globalization is a manifestation of worldwide capitalist expansion, but it involves a multitude of spheres within which it operates. These are economic, social, political, ideological, cultural, and environmental, to mention the most central. However, all of these spheres function within the class configurations of the prevailing social system and have immense political implications.

Economic

I have already pointed out the economic essence of globalization as profit making on a global scale. Here, the central dynamic is capital and its accumulation in private hands throughout the world. The export of capital by the transnational corporations of the advanced capitalist countries to the Third World and elsewhere in the world for control of labor and resources of these regions has historically been part of the process of imperialist expansion worldwide that has led to the growth of giant capitalist conglomerates, cartels, and trusts that have come to dominate the world economy over the course of the twentieth century (Magdoff 1969, 1978, 1992; Amin 1997, 2001). The accelerated rate of exploitation of labor through the expanded reproduction of surplus value (profits) on a world scale facilitates the rapid accumulation of capital by the transnationals at global proportions, a process that stimulates further capital accumulation worldwide, hence further economic domination by the transnationals (Maitra 1996; Siebert 2000; Munck 2002; Sklair 2002). It is this economic essence of globalization, then, that sets into motion the social, political, and ideological contexts in which capitalism prospers.

Social

In the social sphere, we find the global expansion of capital as transforming social relations of production from precapitalist or semicapitalist ones to capitalist ones, where the main class contradictions become wage-labor and capital. The transformation of class relations through this process in a capitalist direction leads to the integration of peripheral countries into the global capitalist economy and the restructuring of the international division of labor for purposes of extracting high rates of profit from superexploited wage-labor (Petras and Veltmeyer 2001). As women workers increasingly constitute the bulk of the low-wage laboring population worldwide, the exploitation of the working class takes on a gender dimension (Barndt 1999; Afshar and Barrientos 1999; Rai 2001; Salazar 2001). The global domination of capital over wage-labor in this process of worldwide capitalist expansion fosters the subordination of the working class to the dictates of transnational capitalists, who not only extract surplus value (profits) from wage-labor, but are also the very source of the emerging inequalities in income, wealth, and power. These inequalities, in time, lead to contradictions and conflict in the social sphere, when class divisions become solidified to a point when class struggles between the opposing class forces begin to surface (Beams 1998).

Political

In the political sphere, power remains in the hands of the capitalist class and is exercised through its "executive committee"—the capitalist state. The transnational capitalist control of the state and major political institutions of society has led to the erosion of bourgeois democracy and to the rise of political corruption (Wallach and Sforza, 1999; Palast 2002; Hertz 2002). However, rather than representing the unified interests of a newly emergent global capitalist class, the state under conditions of globalization continues to protect and advance the interests of "its own" monopoly capitalists, as against other capitalists, for supremacy over the global capitalist economy (Cohn, McBride, and Wiseman 2000; Halliday 2001). Hence, despite a temporary commercial, monetary, and even military union, the leading imperialist state (currently the United States) continues to dominate the world political economy and dictates its terms over other capitalist states, including its chief imperialist rivals, thus giving rise to interimperialist competition and rivalry between the major global capitalist powers (Yang 1995; Hook and Harukiyo 2001; Weber 2001). While this competition takes place at the monopoly level, between rival transnational corporations as well as their states, it nevertheless affects the structure of social relations in general and has a direct impact on other sectors of society as well.

Ideological

In the ideological sphere, global capitalism continues to propagate the superiority of capitalism and "free markets" in a private economy (Rao 1998), emphasizing the "victory" of capitalism over socialism and criticizing the public sphere as inefficient and undesirable—ideas that are a direct reflection of the class interests of the capitalist class. Such ideological propaganda disseminated by the capitalist media and the capitalist state was especially effective in the aftermath of the collapse of the Soviet Union and the East European socialist states, where capitalist practices are making headway (Zloch-Christy 1998). However, as the power and legitimacy of capitalism and profit making come under attack, as harmful to millions of working people around the world, the ideology behind globalization is bound to face opposition from the popular forces advocating an alternative to capitalism, imperialism, and globalization (i.e., the kind of opposition that took place, for example, in the protests and demonstrations against the World Trade Organization [WTO] in Seattle in November 1999, the International Monetary Fund [IMF] and the World Bank in Washington, D.C., in April 2000, and similar such protests in Europe and the United States in 2001 and 2002 [see Starr 2001; Smith and Johnston 2002; Katsiaficas and Yuen 2002]).

Cultural

In the cultural sphere, globalization fosters cultural imperialism (Petras and Bay 1990). This aspect of the global expansion of capital involves the imposition of capitalist cultural values on other precapitalist or noncapitalist societies to integrate them into the world capitalist system. The significance of the transformation of belief systems and cultural practices under the globalization project is such that the dominant values promoted by globalization (such as "privatization" and "free markets"—code words for capitalism) become the new values that are adopted by societies around the world (Falk 1999). Such values are easily translated into consumerism, private accumulation, and other individualistic practices, rather than cooperation and collective/communal values that foster socialism. Thus, the globalization of capital is able in this way to promote the globalization of capitalist values and capitalist culture to legitimize the capitalist system on a worldwide basis (Halliday 2001).

Environmental

Finally, considering the impact of globalization on the environment, the destruction of the ecosystem and the living space (through pollution, contamination, and disposal) to reduce the cost of production has meant the gradual deterioration of the quality of air, water, and soil, with long-range negative consequences that are quite often irreversible (French 2000; Clapp 2001; Lofdahl 2002). While capitalism and the private accumulation of capital has in this way brought about the decline in the quality of the environment, the globalization of capital has accelerated this process and has led to an ecological crisis. In their reckless drive for private accumulation, the transnational corporations have turned much of the world into a dumping ground for the sole purpose of maximizing profits (Karliner 1997). These profits have benefited only a small segment of the world's population while ruining the lives of billions of people throughout the globe. The destruction of the environment through this process has also meant the destruction of the lives and livelihoods of working people the world over and placed the future of our planet into great risk (French 2000; Mol 2001).

THE IMPACT OF GLOBALIZATION ON THE WORKING CLASS

The globalization process has had a direct impact on the working class through the exploitation of labor on a world scale. This has occurred through the restructuring of the international division of labor, which has greatly impacted workers in the Third World, in the advanced capitalist countries, and now in Eastern Europe and the former Soviet Union. Let me outline this impact very briefly as it pertains to the condition of labor in each of these three regions.

The Third World

The impact of globalization on the working class in the Third World has been dramatic. Serving as a source of cheap labor for the production activities of the transnational monopolies, the workers in the Third World have paid a heavy price through high rates of exploitation that they have been subjected to in the global division of labor (Munck 2002). The most prominent of these is the sweatshop conditions in the international garment industry, where workers earn as little as $3 a day producing some of the top label designer clothing that generates high rates of profit for the wealthy owners of the transnationals based in the advanced capitalist countries (Rosen 2002). Lack of basic facilities, poor working conditions, exposure to toxic chemicals, extremely low wages, and lack of basic human rights are some of the most common experiences of workers employed by the transnationals that dominate and control the global economy (Ross 1997). The problems of working people employed at these lowest levels are compounded by high unemployment, underdevelopment, and mass poverty that push living standards down to outright destitution (Wagner 2000).

The sweatshop conditions, exposed by progressive groups, are only one aspect of this mass worldwide exploitation that enriches the capitalists on the one hand and impoverishes the workers on the other. Other, more pervasive forms of class domination and control over the social, political, and economic spheres of society subordinate the interests of the workers to the dictates of the World Trade Organization (WTO), the International Monetary Fund (IMF), the World Bank, and other agencies that foster the global agenda of transnational capital whose interests are diametrically opposed to that of labor. But, beyond their direct exploitation at the point of production, workers, as consumers, also face a multitude of problems that are directly traceable to the globalization process (Beams 1998).

This is the case because the globalization project fostered by imperialism and the imperialist states takes place within the context of a global economy within which the transnational corporations are the chief proponents of the move toward privatization—one that directly benefits the largest and most powerful corporations at the expense of the rest of society, especially the working people by whose labor these transnationals prosper.

The reality of the situation is that the globalization process hurts the working people and enriches the capitalists. It marginalizes the workers and the masses in general and worsens their already deplorable working conditions. It turns the Third World into one giant sweatshop in which workers sweat to produce a myriad of products destined for markets in the advanced capitalist countries (Ross 1997).

The marginalization of the working people in the Third World takes place through the deterioration of living conditions in both the rural and urban areas. In the rural areas, peasants are uprooted and driven off the land by big landowners to make way for the transnational agricultural conglomerates, with the result that the mass migration to urban areas have increased the number of unemployed and working poor in a much more accelerated pace than before—a situation that has led to a massive increase in the poverty population. This problem is compounded by the prevalence of cheap, semi-slave contract-labor working under deplorable working conditions—a factor that has exacerbated the problem of poverty in the Third World (Amaladoss 1999). This, in turn, has led to enormous income inequalities, hence a tremendous widening of the gap between the capitalist rich and the working poor. These conditions faced by working people throughout the Third World are the result of the development of capitalism over the course of the twentieth century, but the onset of globalization and worldwide imperialist expansion has exacerbated this situation even more so, and on a world scale, in direct proportion to the growth and expansion of capitalism throughout the world.

In short, the aim of globalization is to turn the entire planet into a giant capitalist enterprise controlled directly from Wall Street and other centers of world capitalism, and to do so with only one thing in mind: profits. But the contradictions inherent in this process inevitably create problems for the system. And these problems surface, again and again, in the form of class struggles (Beams 1998).

The Advanced Capitalist Countries

While the globalization process hurts working people the most in the Third World, it also hurts the interests of the working people in the advanced capitalist countries. The globalization of capital and capitalist expansion abroad has had immense dislocations in the national economies of imperialist states. The transfer of manufacturing abroad has meant a decline in local industrial production, as plant closings in the United States and other advanced capitalist countries have worsened the unemployment and underemployment situation (Phillips 1998). The massive expansion of capital worldwide has resulted in hundreds of factory shutdowns with millions of workers losing their jobs or taking up employment in the low-wage service sector in both the United States and other imperialist states. This has led to a decline in wages of workers in the advanced capitalist centers, as low wages abroad have played a competitive role in keeping wages down in the imperialist heartlands. The drop in income among a growing section of the working class has thus lowered the standard of living in general and led to a further polarization between labor and capital (Tonelson 2000).

As conditions deteriorate for working people in the imperial center, and as the restructuring of the global economy proceeds with increasing speed, leaving behind a disaffected working class that is becoming increasingly impoverished and destitute, the potential for a renewed labor activism and struggle increases and makes it possible for working people around the world to share their experiences and build bonds toward greater understanding of their position, interests, and potential for struggle against the global capitalist system (Waterman 1998; Houtart and Polet 2001). This struggle, which increasingly becomes political over time, evolves into a struggle between labor and capital at global proportions. Therein lies the possibility of a renewed international solidarity of labor that leads to new forms of struggle and resistance on a worldwide basis (Foran 2002).

Eastern Europe and the Former Soviet Union

In the period since the collapse of the former socialist states of Eastern Europe and the Soviet Union, transnational capital has expanded its global reach to penetrate various countries of this region that were previously closed or regulated through state controls that limited external influence on their economy, state, and society (Kozul-Wright and Rowthorn 1998). The most glaring example of this expansion has been the wholesale takeover of the former German Democratic Republic by West German capital. But the penetration of

Western capital into other former socialist states of Eastern Europe has proceeded in full speed, most visibly in Hungary, Poland, the Czech Republic, and the Baltic states of the former Soviet Union. In these and other more developed regions of Eastern Europe, foreign capital has concentrated on large-scale manufacturing production using cheap labor to produce products destined for both the local market and those in the advanced capitalist countries (Zloch-Christy 1998). The employment of cheap labor and the capture of local emerging consumer markets has generated enormous levels of profit and led to control over labor and local resources through joint ventures with Western capital and government giveaways by way of privatization of the local economy—a situation that has created enormous dislocation of the economy and society, with human and ecological consequences (Manser 1994). In these more advanced states of Eastern Europe, it has been the workers who have suffered the most through low wages and high rates of exploitation that have generated enormous levels of profit for the transnationals and their local capitalist collaborators, who also have benefited from their presence through the appropriation of a portion of the profits, as well as through bureaucratic mismanagement and corruption (Callinicos 1991; Simon 2000).

Elsewhere in Eastern Europe, such as in Romania, Bulgaria, and other less developed countries of the region, and in some former Soviet republics, such as Azerbaijan, Turkmenistan, and other republics in Central Asia, transnational capital has concentrated on raw materials production, including oil in the Caspian Sea region, agricultural raw materials in countries bordering the Black Sea, and metals and minerals in the Siberian region of Russia. In these and other regions of Eastern Europe and the former Soviet Union where foreign capital has made limited investments to utilize human resources, the focus on raw materials exports has turned these regions into appendages of the world economy not unlike the neocolonial regimes of the Third World that came to serve global capitalist interests in the latter part of the twentieth century (Maitra 1996). Today, the former socialist states of Eastern Europe and the Soviet Union are serving the same interests at the cost of enormous human misery to the great majority of the population of these countries who now live in outright poverty and destitution (Atal 1999; Emigh and Szelenyi 2000).

GLOBALIZATION AND ITS TRANSFORMATION: CLASS STRUGGLE AND THE PROSPECTS FOR CHANGE

Looking at the class contradictions of the globalization process and the prospects for change in the world situation, one notes the resurgence of renewed anti-imperialist struggles through the formation of new revolutionary social movements in the Third World during this latest phase of globalization (e.g., the Zapatistas in Chiapas) and the radicalization of the labor movement in the advanced capitalist countries and the development of protest movements in mainland Europe, Britain, and increasingly North America (Starr 2001; Houtart and Polet 2001; Smith and Johnston 2002; Yuen, Katsiaficas, and Rose 2002).

Unlike in earlier periods of anti-imperialist mobilization, however, when nationalism was the defining characteristic of the radical anti-imperialist movements, today popular movements in the Third World are led by the working class and its organizations. As a result, the struggle against globalization in the Third World is moving beyond the anti-imperialist struggle and taking on more and more an anticapitalist character (Petras 1998; Starr 2001; Yuen, Katsiaficas, and Rose 2002). This is so because labor unions and other workers' organizations have increasingly taken the lead to initiate the kinds of mass movements that will evolve into a wider global effort to unite labor across national boundaries, so that a broader global unity of the working class can be built on a worldwide basis (Munck and Waterman 1999; Munck 2002; Nissen 2002).

Similar to developments in the Third World, in the advanced capitalist countries, too, there has been a resurgence of the labor movement, and workers' organizations (primarily labor unions in the United States and labor unions and workers' political parties in Europe and elsewhere) have taken the lead to mobilize workers to address the problems created by globalization in the heartlands of the global economy (Smith and Johnston 2002). While these movements are stronger and play a more direct role in Europe and Britain, the move toward greater mobilization of labor to rally workers' support in the United States is becoming an important aspect of the struggle against globalization and the global project of the transnationals—and increasingly on the very soil where their global reach took root. It is thus at the home base of the transnationals where we will more and more witness the kinds of opposition that is beginning to develop against them (Katsiaficas and Yuen 2002).

These and other developments engendered by the globalization process lead one to the inescapable conclusion that the contradictions of the global political economy will result in increased class struggles in the years ahead, with the potential development of radical social transformations that are yet to come.

Chapter One

Theories of the Global Economy and Global Empire

Various attempts have been made to explain the rise and demise of the major world powers from earlier times to the present, and many competing explanations have been provided to account for the success and failure of states that have risen to world prominence and established global empires over long historical periods. The Spanish, the Dutch, the French, the British, and more recently the United States and other global and regional powers since the sixteenth century are cited as dominant global economic, political, and military empires that established themselves as the preeminent centers of the global power structure, with enormous impact on both their rivals and the world at large, as well as their internal economic, political, military, and, ultimately, societal structure. What has been less than satisfactory, however, are the limited answers provided by various theories on the nature and causes of the rise and fall of empires in the world historical context.

In this opening chapter, I examine a number of different approaches that explain the origins, nature, development, and contradictions of global empires in an effort to delineate the various positions on this question and thus guide us in our attempt to explain the legacy of the U.S. empire in the present global political-economic context.

In broad outlines, we can distinguish three major approaches in studies of the global economy and global empires that explain the expansion and contraction of the great imperial powers in recent history: (1) the liberal approach, (2) the world-system approach, and (3) the Marxist approach. I take up each of these approaches and briefly discuss their theoretical positions and methods of analysis within the context of global power relations.

THE LIBERAL APPROACH

The liberal approach to the study of the global political economy is best ex-
emplified by the analysis provided in Paul Kennedy's book *The Rise and Fall
of the Great Powers* (1987). In it, Kennedy makes a compelling argument in
favor of a political-military theory of empire within the context of an analysis of global power relations affected by economic changes and their impact
on an empire's relative position in the world order.

Referring to the history of the Western powers since the sixteenth century,
Kennedy argues that "there is a very clear connection *in the long run* between
an individual Great Power's economic rise and fall and its growth and decline
as an important military power (or world empire)" (1987, xii). For Kennedy,
the critical factor determining "the rise and fall of the Great Powers" is that
the dominant world powers/empires "steadily overextend themselves in the
course of repeated conflicts and become militarily top-heavy for their weakening economic base":

> In these more troubled circumstances, the Great Power is likely to find itself spend-
> ing much *more* on defense than it did two generations earlier, and yet still discover
> that the world is a less secure environment—simply because other Powers have
> grown faster, and are becoming stronger. . . . Great Powers in relative decline in-
> stinctively respond by spending more on "security," and thereby divert potential re-
> sources from "investment" and compound their long-term dilemma. (1987, xxiii)

As a result of such military overextension, which drains productive resources of a nation and brings about an economic decline, a great power increasingly runs the risk of being replaced by rival states that do not have such
a military burden and are thus in a better economic position to overtake and
surpass a declining empire. In fact, it is precisely in this way, according to
Kennedy, that shifts in global power centers occur and transformations in the
world political economy take place:

> An economically expanding Power—Britain in the 1860s, the United States in
> the 1890s, Japan today—may well prefer to become rich rather than to spend
> heavily on armaments. A half-century later, priorities may well have altered. The
> earlier economic expansion has brought with it overseas obligations (depen-
> dence upon foreign markets and raw materials, military alliances, perhaps bases
> and colonies). Other, rival Powers are now economically expanding at a faster
> rate, and wish in their turn to extend their influence abroad. (1987, xiii)

Finally, the burden of military spending to maintain a global empire becomes more serious, and the decline and fall of a state from empire status that

much more likely, if the state in question is also experiencing a relative economic decline, "If a state overextends itself strategically—by, say, . . . the
waging of costly wars—it runs the risk that the potential benefits from external expansion may be outweighed by the great expense of it all—a dilemma
which becomes acute if the nation concerned has entered a period of relative
economic decline" (Kennedy 1987, xvi). While an empire requires a suffi-
ciently large economic base to sustain its political-military power and to remain a dominant force on the world scene, it is ultimately the overextended
projection of strategic military force, with all the economic costs it entails,
and with it a corresponding decline in the economy itself, that finally brings
about the decline and fall of a global empire, according to Kennedy. Thus, "a
top-heavy military establishment may slow down the rate of economic
growth and lead to a decline in the nation's share of world manufacturing
output, and therefore wealth, and therefore *power* . . . a dilemma which becomes *acute* if the nation concerned has entered *a period of relative economic
decline*" (1987, 445, xvi, emphasis added).

This simple, yet provocative, explanation of the world historical process
confronting the major world powers today—such as the United States, with
its large-scale military intervention in the Middle East, precisely at a time
when the U.S. economy has entered a deep recession—is both instructive and
timely. It also provides a framework for analysis of the U.S. economy and
polity and the role of military spending vis-à-vis the structural problems of
the U.S. economy and the state in this period of decline and decay.[1]

However, as in other liberal political accounts of the global political economy, Kennedy's approach, focusing as it does on the nation-state as the main
unit of analysis, seriously limits our understanding of the nature and causes
of global conflicts, rivalry, and shifts in power that can otherwise be more
clearly delineated by an analysis of classes and class conflicts lodged in particular nation-states. Restricted to an empirical-descriptive diplomatic history
of the world political situation shaped by the general concepts of nations and
empires and defined in geographic, political-military terms—albeit affected
by economic changes, but divorced from an understanding of the logic of a
historically specific dominant mode of production as ultimately determining
the nature, scope, and extent of an empire's political-military superstructure
and its global dynamics—Kennedy's liberal-institutional approach fails to
provide an analysis of the real forces behind the surface manifestations of political behavior of states/empires at the global level.

In the absence of the application of a theory of economic systems to define states in accordance with their socioeconomic base in production, or, for
that matter, by any other definition, Kennedy's universalist treatment of

states/empires divorced from historical time and space leads him to lump Ming China, Tokugawa Japan, Ottoman Turkey, France, Britain, Germany, the United States, the Soviet Union, and present-day Japan and China, as well as all other major political-military powers, past and present, into the same category, with some—the most powerful and prominent—given great power status, without regard to their socioeconomic systems or relations of production or the class nature of the state.

Kennedy's central argument, revolving around the military element explaining the rise and fall of empires, thus forces him to look at these states in the same way, hoping to find a uniformity of causation in factors contributing to their decline and fall and in the process failing to explain the systemic reasons for each case that is socially and historically specific. By failing to see that global military expansion of the Western powers as a manifestation of economic expansion by the capitalist class internationally and that the globalization of capital leads to the establishment of worldwide economic domination by the capitalist monopolies, which in turn necessitates the capitalist state to expand its political-military influence and action internationally in order to protect the interests of its capitalist class, thus establishing itself as a global empire, Kennedy characterizes the world order as an "anarchical" one wherein "egoistical" nation-states fight it out in endless wars for world supremacy. Thus, given their common logic—the struggle for power—what determines the success or failure of these states now turned global empires, according to Kennedy, is the degree to which they can balance their military ambitions with the reality of their available economic resources. A disparity between the two, resulting in military overexpansion, is a formula for failure—one that signals long-term decline and demise. However, Kennedy fails to see that international economic expansion of a given state (which leads to increased military expenditures to defend its global interests) would, in turn, adversely affect its domestic economy on which it depends for further military spending to sustain the empire. Thus, he fails to see that the global expansion and relocation of monopoly capital (causing a reduction in the size and strength of the domestic economy, hence its ability to support an overextended military on a world scale) is the *real* reason for decline and fall of empire.[2]

Starting his analysis in an inverted order, Kennedy fails to tell us why an empire would overextend itself militarily in the first place and inflict on itself economic disaster, thus running the risk of being replaced by a global rival. One would like to know: Who are the dominant forces that are pushing for such military expansion and why? Although it may ruin the economy of an entire nation, who (which social class) might benefit from such military expansion? That the logic of an economic system and the class forces that control it may well be the driving force of such action, and not the "preferences," "priorities," or "wishes" of states, as Kennedy would have it, never occurs to him as the decisive factor explaining, in the end, the rise and fall of the great powers in the world today.

THE WORLD-SYSTEM APPROACH

In contrast to the liberal tradition in political theory, Immanuel Wallerstein provides an alternative world-system approach for an analysis of the global political economy. Explaining his method in selecting the world system as the unit of analysis, rather than the nation or the state, Wallerstein argues that he "abandoned the idea altogether of taking either the sovereign state or that vaguer concept, the national society, as the unit of analysis. I decided that neither one was a social system and that one could only speak of social change in social systems. The only social system in this scheme was the world system" (1974a, 7). "Once we assume that the unit of analysis is such a world system and not the state or the nation or the people," he argues, "then much changes in the outcome of the analysis. Most specifically we shift from a concern with the attributive characteristics of states to concern with the relational characteristics of states. We shift from seeing classes (and status groups) as groups within a state to seeing them as groups within a world-economy" (Wallerstein 1989, xi).

Going beyond the liberal political tradition and conceptualizing global power struggles as those in accordance with the requirements of a world system that dominates the global political economy over an entire historical period, the world-system approach attempts to provide tools of analysis to examine contemporary global political-military developments in the context of the logic of the capitalist world economy that has come to dominate the structure of economic relations on a world scale since the sixteenth century.

The capitalist world economy, defined in terms of market and exchange relations, which binds states under its yoke across the globe, brings capitalist and noncapitalist states alike under its sway and determines the nature and course of these states' development as dictated by the most powerful state in control of the world system in a given historical epoch. But competition and rivalry between the leading states engaged in struggle for domination of the world system leave open the possibility that a dominant state in a given historical epoch will be replaced by another:

> While the advantages of the core-states have not ceased to expand throughout the history of the modern world-system, the ability of a particular state to remain in the core sector is not beyond challenge. The hounds are ever to the hares for

the position of top dog. Indeed, it may well be that in this kind of system it is not structurally possible to avoid, over a long period of historical time, a circulation of elites in the sense that the particular country that is dominant at a given time tends to be replaced in this role sooner or later by another country. (Wallerstein 1974b, 350)

Moving beyond nation-states and formulating the problem in world systemic terms, Wallerstein provides an alternative explanation of the rise and fall of world systems, which take place in much longer historical periods and constitute the very basis of world historical transformations.

In "The Rise and Future Demise of the World Capitalist System" (1974b), Wallerstein argues in favor of just such a conceptualization in explaining the origins, development, and future transformation of the capitalist world economy and system. Likewise, situating the problematic in a broader historical context of systemic transformation, Wallerstein, in *The Modern World-System* (1974a), attempts to explain the transition from feudalism to capitalism in western Europe and the subsequent rise of the capitalist system in such world systemic terms.

An essential element in the global analysis of the modern world system is the theory's three-tiered model of "core," "periphery," and "semiperiphery," which divides the world system into three areas or zones that are defined on the basis of a society's level of development and incorporation into the world system. Moreover, the political-economic content of such incorporation determines whether a given social formation is part of the core, the periphery, or the semiperiphery (Wallerstein 1974a, 1974b). "The organizing principle of this operation is the categorical differentiation of levels of the world system: core, semiperiphery, and periphery. These zones, distinguished by their different economic functions within the world-economic division of labor . . . structure the assemblage of productive processes that constitute the capitalist world-economy" (Hopkins and Wallerstein 1981, 77). "On a world-scale," continue Terence K. Hopkins and Wallerstein, "the processes of the division of labor that define and integrate the world-economy are . . . those which we designate as 'core' and 'periphery'" (1981, 45). Moreover, "although obviously derivative from the core-periphery conception," they add, "there exists a third category, structurally distinct from core and periphery": "Looking at the world-economy as a whole, . . . [there exists] a basically triadic world-scale division of labor among, now, core states, semiperipheral states, and peripheral areas" (47). Thus, "the world-economy became basically structured as an increasingly interrelated system of strong 'core' and weak 'peripheral' states, in which interstate relations . . . are continually shaped and in turn continually shape the deepening and expanding world-scale division and integration of production" (43).

This brings up the question of "the network(s) of governance or rule in the area in question." "In this respect," write Hopkins and Wallerstein, "incorporation entails the expansion of the world-economy's interstate system":

> Interstate relations, and the interstate system overall, in part express and in part circumscribe or structure the world-scale accumulation/production process. In short, the relational networks forming the interstate system are integral to, not outside of, the networks constitutive of the social economy defining the scope and reach of the modern world-system. . . .
>
> Insofar as external areas are incorporated, then—and in the singular development of the modern world-system all have been—the transition period framing incorporation encloses definite directions of change in a once external area's arrangements and processes of rule or governance. (1981, 245–246)

The main feature of the modern world system is, in essence, the transfer of surplus from the periphery to the core of the system, conceptualized in a manner similar to the Frankian "metropolis-satellite" model of domination and "exploitation." The mechanism whereby this transfer takes place is "unequal exchange"—a mechanism made possible by the domination of peripheral states by those in the core:

> Once we get a difference in the strength of the state machineries, we get the operation of "unequal exchange" which is enforced by strong states on weak ones, by core states on peripheral areas. Thus capitalism involves not only appropriation of the surplus value by an owner from a laborer, but an appropriation of surplus of the whole-world-economy by core areas. And this was as true in the stage of agricultural capitalism as it is in the stage of industrial capitalism. (Wallerstein 1979, 18–19)

More specifically, Wallerstein argues that without this process of "unequal exchange" the capitalist world economy could not exist, "Such a system [of unequal exchange] is *necessary* for the expansion of a world market if the primary consideration is *profit*. Without *unequal* exchange, it would not be *profitable* to expand the size of the division of labor. And without such expansion, it would not be profitable to maintain a capitalist world-economy, which would then either disintegrate or revert to the form of a redistributive world-empire" (1979, 71).

Despite the subordination of peripheral states to those in the core, and the exploitation of the former by the latter through surplus extraction, the modern world system allows, under certain conditions and in the context of certain political-economic processes, the transformation of some peripheral states into semiperipheral ones. However, such transformation (or mobility) of states along the three-tiered continuum takes place within the context and logic of the system as a whole and as a consequence of the dictates of the dominant world system in a given historical period. Thus, the various parts of the system that make up its totality always function within the framework of the relationship of the parts to the whole.

Although Wallerstein's world-system approach is certainly a major improvement over Kennedy's ahistorical eclecticism, it nevertheless suffers from a number of fundamental flaws that must be pointed out. The first, and central, flaw of this approach is the treatment of the world system in strictly circulationist terms. Capitalism, defined as a system of accumulation for profit through the market, is conceptualized in the context of exchange relations. Thus, economic relations take place between states within the context of such market exchange. As a result, the question of the mode of production and the relations of production, its social component, are ignored or eliminated from analysis, such that class relations and class struggles based on relations of production also disappear as irrelevant. We are thus left with the generalized abstract notions of "world system" and "world economy" consisting of the three zones (core, periphery, and semiperiphery) between which all the major global relations and conflicts take place. And since changes in any of these three zones, by themselves, cannot bring changes in the world economy or the system as a whole, the system, in all its totality and static abstraction, becomes an end in itself—in effect, an ideal-typical construct studied for its own sake.[3]

Having criticized the great powers approach for its universalism and ahistorical eclecticism with regard to the sources of power and politics in the world political economy, we now find ourselves confronting the equally universalist and ahistorical static abstractions of the world-systems approach, which has taken us far along an analysis of the broader systemic logic of the capitalist world economy, but not near enough to its class contradictions and conflicts that would provide us the clues to the underlying dialectical class structure and class logic of the empire and its legacy. For this, we must turn to the Marxist approach.

THE MARXIST APPROACH

In response to the deficiencies of both the liberal-political and world-system approaches examined earlier, there has recently emerged a third, Marxist approach in critical theorizing on the nature of the state, empire, and imperialism. While there are numerous prominent examples of this approach in contemporary political economy surrounding the debate on imperialism and the state on a world scale during the past three decades, I focus on the analysis provided by Albert Szymanski in *The Logic of Imperialism* (1981) as representative of works written in this class-analysis tradition.

"The motive force behind capitalist imperialism," writes Szymanski, "is found to be the maximization of profits by the transnational corporations that dominate the foreign relations of the major capitalist states" (1981, 123). "These giant corporations and banks are able to transform their tremendous domestic and international wealth into political power, turning the state into an instrument that guarantees their profits" (147). Thus, the international role of the dominant imperialist states are centered on preserving a general climate favorable to profitable investment and trade and is oriented to advancing the interests of the imperialist system as a whole. Moreover, the "various forms of military intervention used by the imperialist states" must, therefore, be seen as "an attempt to ensure the interests of the transnational corporations" (177). Thus, "to secure the profits of empire . . . a strong world military presence is required that can suppress or intimidate attempts to arouse socialist or nationalist revolutions" (517). In this way, the supremacy of the imperialist state and transnational capital can be ensured throughout the empire.

The relationship between the owners of the transnationals—the monopoly capitalist class—and the imperialist state and the role and functions of this state, including the use of military force to advance the interests of the monopoly capitalist class, thus reveals the class nature of the imperialist state and the class logic of imperialist expansion on a world scale. But, as Szymanski points out, this logic is more pervasive and is based on the logic of a more fundamental class relation between labor and capital that now operates on a global scale, that is, a relation based on exploitation. Thus, in the epoch of capitalist imperialism, "classes," writes Szymanski, "are a product of the logic of the world capitalist system":

It is the logic of the relationship between the international capitalist class and the working class . . . that is the primary cause of social structures, political forms, and their transformations.

The logic of classes generally explains the actions of nation-states. . . . Class logic is, in the last analysis, the fundamental integrating force in any world system. . . . [Thus,] classes, not nations, must be considered the most fundamental active units of world systems. (1981, 15–16)

This position is echoed by James Petras in *Critical Perspectives on Imperialism and Social Class in the Third World,* where he writes:

> The capitalist world market thus must be demystified from a set of static institutions/factors and described essentially for what it is: a series of class relationships that have their anchorage and instrumentation in the imperialist states. The world market operates through the class-directed institutions that impose the exploitative class relationship throughout the world. The world capitalist system can best be analyzed by examining the hegemonic class relationship and imperialist state and conflicting class relationships that emerge in each formation. (1978, 39)

Thus, "it is out of these class relationships and the power of the contending classes," Petras writes elsewhere, "that the integration/disintegration of the imperial system originates" (1981, 8). Hence, "the more centrally the class struggle affects the overall functioning of the imperial system, the more absolute dependence between state and class structure": "The image of the imperial state standing above the class structure that organizes imperialist wars in fact disguises the greatest concentration of social power into the executive agencies of the imperial state and the subordination of civil society to the organized power of the imperial capitalist class" (10–11). It is for this reason, Petras stresses, that "the critical problem for analysis is . . . one of examining the conditions under which the process of capital accumulation takes place and its impact on the class structure. Class relations are viewed as a point of departure within which to locate the problem of capital accumulation and expansion" (37).

Explaining the class logic of global capitalist expansion in the twentieth century, "Imperialism," writes Szymanski, "involves the exploitation of the producer or working classes in the dominated country by economic interests based in the dominating country" (1981, 6). And the mechanism that facilitates this exploitation is foreign investment (in raw materials and, increasingly, in manufacturing), which, by way of cheap labor and raw materials, obtains high rates of profit for the transnational monopolies based in the advanced capitalist countries:

> Foreign investment is immensely profitable for the transnational corporations. It is in such profitability that the motive behind imperialism is found. . . .
>
> The tremendous profits made by the transnational corporations in the raw materials sector (especially petroleum) . . . come mostly from their monopoly power in the world market. . . .
>
> The rapidly increasing profits made in the manufacturing sector . . . come from the utilization of extremely cheap labor. . . .

In most less-developed capitalist countries authoritarian regimes outlaw or greatly inhibit strikes, independent unions, and other forms of working class resistance. Such regimes thus provide the transnational corporations with both a cheap and responsive labor force. (133–137)

Thus, imperialism has been an enormous source of profit and wealth for the capitalist class of the advanced capitalist countries, who, through the mechanisms of the transnational monopolies and the imperial state, have accumulated great fortunes from the exploitation of labor on a world scale.

Given the uneven development of capitalism, however, some countries have grown more rapidly than others, while previously less developed countries have emerged as new centers of world capitalism. The rivalry between the capitalist classes of the old and newly emergent capitalist states has turned into rivalry among the leading countries within the world capitalist system. This has led to intense competition and conflict between the rising capitalist powers and the declining imperial centers on a world scale, hence leading to shifts in centers of global economic and political power.

The process of global capitalist expansion discussed earlier has produced a number of major consequences, which are examined at length in this book and elsewhere (see Berberoglu 1987b, 1992a, 2001; see also Petras and Veltmeyer 2001). These can be listed briefly as follows:

1. The globalization of capital and the development of capitalism and capitalist relations of production in the less developed countries resulting in the superexploitation of a growing working class
2. The rise of new capitalist centers on the world scene (e.g., Japan, Germany, and the European Union), thus leading to interimperialist rivalry
3. The necessity to protect and police the empire, hence the procurement and maintenance of a large number of military bases around the world, frequent military intervention in the Third World, and, as a result, an enormous increase in military spending
4. Decline of the domestic economy and a reduction in the living standard of U.S. workers, leading to increased class polarization
5. The class contradictions of imperialism and capitalist development on a world scale, preparing the material conditions for intensified class struggles that lead to revolutionary social transformations throughout the world, including the empire's home base

Focusing on the U.S. experience, it is clear that in the post–World War II period the United States emerged as the dominant power in the capitalist world. In subsequent decades, U.S.-controlled transnational production reached a decisive stage, necessitating the restructuring of the international division of labor, as the export of productive capital effected a shift in the nature and location of production: the expansion of manufacturing industry on an unprecedented scale into previously precapitalist, peripheral areas of the global capitalist economy. This marked a turning point in the rise to world prominence of the U.S. economy and the emergence of the United States as the leading capitalist/imperialist power in the world.

NOTES

1. The argument of the negative impact of excessive military spending on the economy is certainly not a new one. A similar argument was made earlier by Seymour Melman in the 1960s (see Melman 1965). For an elaboration of this theme, in the context of the growing relationship between the economy and the military establishment, see Melman (1970).

2. Thus, "the rise and fall of empires" in this context can be seen as nothing other than the rise and fall of capitalist classes of rival economic powers across the world. Political-military overextension, therefore, can be seen as an outcome of the underlying economic struggles among competing capitalist classes at the global level. Inter-imperialist rivalry is thus based not on political or military power and supremacy per se, but on economic strength among rival propertied classes to possess the greatest share of economic wealth in the world. It is only within this economic context that political and military power must be situated. For, as Kennedy would agree, it is the states with the strongest economies incurring the least amount of military expenditure and force (e.g., Germany and Japan today) that would win out in the global struggle for empire status.

3. Going a step further, James Petras correctly observes that "without a clear notion of the antagonistic class interests located in the interior of a social formation, there is a tendency among world-system theorists to dissolve the issue into a series of abstract developmental imperatives deduced from a static global stratification system which increasingly resembles the functional requisites and equilibrium models of Parsonian sociology" (1978, 37).

Chapter Two

The Logic of Global Capitalist Expansion: Theories of Modern Imperialism

The central figures associated with the theory of capitalist imperialism are John A. Hobson, Rosa Luxemburg, and V. I. Lenin. The most authoritative of all Marxist studies of imperialism, however, is Lenin's *Imperialism: The Highest Stage of Capitalism* ([1917] 1975). This work, incorporating the work of numerous Marxist and non-Marxist writers, is regarded by most Marxists today as the definitive statement of classic Marxist theory of capitalist imperialism. Before delving into Lenin's book, however, it is first necessary to discuss the work of his predecessors. I begin the discussion with an examination of the work of the eminent British economist John A. Hobson, whose book *Imperialism: A Study* ([1905] 1972) played a key role in the formulation of much of the arguments developed by Lenin (although Lenin, of course, reached substantially different conclusions than the social-liberal Hobson).

HOBSON'S THEORY

"Imperialism," wrote Hobson at the turn of the twentieth century, "implies the use of the machinery of government by private interests, mainly capitalist, to secure for them economic gains outside their country" ([1905] 1972, 94). He argued that

> [t]he economic root of Imperialism is the desire of strong organized industrial and financial interests to secure and develop at the public expense and by the public force private markets for their surplus goods and their surplus capital. . . .
> Imperialism—whether it consists in a further policy of expansion or in the rigorous maintenance of all those vast tropical lands which have been earmarked

as British spheres of influence—implies militarism now and ruinous wars in the future. . . .

This truth is now for the first time brought sharply and nakedly before the mind of the nation. (106, 130)

The main purpose of Hobson's study was to demonstrate that the new imperialism had an insignificant commercial value and that therefore it was "an irrational and unnecessary policy":

The absorption of so large a proportion of public interest, energy, blood and money in seeking to procure colonial possessions and foreign markets would seem to indicate that Great Britain obtained her chief livelihood by external trade. Now this was not the case. Large as was our foreign and colonial trade in volume and in value, essential as was much of it to our national well-being, nevertheless it furnished a small proportion of the total industry of the nation.

. . . The distinctive feature of modern Imperialism, from the commercial standpoint, is that it adds to our empire tropical and subtropical regions with which our trade is small, precarious and unprogressive. . . .

The entire volume of our export trade with our new protectorates in Africa, Asia and the Pacific . . . forms an utterly insignificant part of our national income, while the expenses connected directly and indirectly with the acquisition, administration and defense of these possessions must swallow an immeasurably larger sum. ([1905] 1972, 28, 38–39)

The new imperialism, according to Hobson, was an unwise policy not only from the standpoint of the British economy and society, but also in terms of its exploitive consequences in the colonies, which aroused the resentment of oppressed people. This concern led Hobson to raise the central question of his study, "How is the British nation induced to embark upon such unsound business?" He had no hesitation in his mind to reply that "the only possible answer is that the business interests of the nation as a whole are subordinated to those of certain sectional interests that usurp control of the national resources and use them for their private gain" ([1905] 1972, 46). "Although the new imperialism has been bad business for the nation," he wrote, "it has been good business for certain classes and certain trades within the nation" (46). And while Britain's imperialist course appears irrational from the point of view of the nation as a whole, an analysis of the relationship between business and politics, he argued, will show that imperialism, viewed from another angle—that is, from that of certain classes who benefit from it—is far more rational than it appears at first sight: "the aggressive Imperialism . . . is not in the main the product of blind passions of races or of the mixed folly and ambition of politicians. It is far more rational than at first sight appears. Irrational from the standpoint of the whole nation, it is rational enough from the standpoint of certain classes in the nation" (47).

The implications of Hobson's analysis thus far leads us to conclude that there exist in the national economy interests that benefit, directly or indirectly, from imperialist expansion and that it is these interests that either initiate or support it. But who are these interests?

Hobson had no hesitation in giving us a full picture of the key interests involved in the perpetuation of Britain's imperialist expansion:

> Certain definite business and professional interests feeding upon imperialistic expenditure, or upon the results of that expenditure, are thus set up in opposition to the common good, and instinctively feeling their way to one another, are found united in strong sympathy to support every new imperialist exploit . . . certain big firms engaged in building warships and transports, equipping and coaling them, manufacturing guns, rifles, ammunition, planes and motor vehicles of every kind, supplying horses, wagons, saddlery, food, clothing for the services, contracting for barracks, and for other large irregular needs. Through these main channels the millions flow to feed many subsidiary trades, most of which are quite aware that they are engaged in executing contracts for the services. Here we have an important nucleus of commercial Imperialism. Some of these trades, especially the shipbuilding, boilermaking and gun and ammunition making trades, are conducted by large firms with immense capital whose heads are well aware of the uses of political influence for trade purposes.
>
> These men are Imperialists by conviction; a pushful policy is good for them.
>
> With them stand the great manufacturers for export trade who gain a living by supplying the real or artificial wants of the new countries we annex or open up. Manchester, Sheffield, Birmingham, to name three representative cases, are full of firms which compete in pushing textiles and hardware, engines, tools, machinery, spirits, and guns upon new markets. The public debts which ripen in our colonies, and in foreign countries that come under our protectorate or influence, are largely loaned in the shape of rails, engines, guns, and other materials of civilization made and sent out by British firms. The making of railways, canals and other public works, the establishment of factories, the development of mines, the improvement of agriculture in new countries, stimulate a definite interest to important manufacturing industries which feeds a very firm imperialist faith in their owners. ([1905] 1972, 49)

In contrast to the small gains from external trade, Britain's global strategy of expansion rested primarily on foreign investment, according to Hobson, "By far the most important economic factor in Imperialism is the influence relating to investments. The growing cosmopolitanism of capital has been the greatest economic change of recent generations. Every advanced industrial nation has been tending to place a larger share of its capital outside the limits of its own political area, in foreign countries, or in colonies, and to draw a growing income from this source" ([1905] 1972, 51).

"The modern foreign policy of Great Britain," stressed Hobson, "has been primarily a struggle for profitable markets of investment." He continued:

> To a larger extent every year Great Britain has been becoming a nation living upon tribute from abroad, and the classes who enjoy this tribute have had an ever-increasing incentive to employ the public policy, the public purse, and the public force to extend the field of their private investments. This is, perhaps, the most important fact in modern politics, and the obscurity in which it is wrapped has constituted the gravest danger to our State. . . . Aggressive Imperialism . . . is a source of great gain to the investor who cannot find at home the profitable use he seeks for his capital and insists that his government should help him to profitable and secure investments abroad. ([1905] 1972, 53–54, 55)

Hobson's analysis of the central interests involved in imperialist expansion undoubtedly rested on the investor. But, as he later pointed out, in order to make the analysis complete it is at least equally important to bring in the special role of the financier and his specific relationship to the investor. "If the special interest of the investor is liable to clash with the public interests and to induce a wrecking policy," he argued, "still more dangerous is the special interest of the financier, the general dealer in investments. . . . These great businesses—banking, brokering, bill discounting, loan floating, company promoting—form the central ganglion of international capitalism" ([1905] 1972, 56). Speaking of the financiers:

> There is not a war, a revolution, an anarchist assassination or any other public shock which is not gainful to these men; they are harpies who suck their gains from every new forced expenditure and every sudden disturbance of public credit.
> . . . [T]he terrible sufferings of England and South Africa in the war . . . has been a source of immense profit to the big financiers who have best held out against the uncalculated waste, and have recouped themselves by profitable war contracts and by "freezing out" the smaller interest in the Transvaal. These men are the only certain gainers from the war, and most of their gains are made out of the public losses of their adopted country or the private losses of their fellow countrymen. (58)

Thus, Hobson argued that considering all the gains and costs of Britain's imperialist policy, it was clearly detrimental to the interests of the nation and the people as a whole. The contradiction of such venture was great gains for a minority involved in foreign investment and finance capital on the one hand and great expenditure of public money on the military on the other.

The public expense in maintaining the empire was so great that this meant movement toward a permanent debt budget for the state. This led Hobson to the conclusion that "the creation of public debts is a normal and a most imposing feature of imperialism." In his words, "The creation of large growing public debts is thus not only a necessary consequence of an imperialist expenditure, too great for its current revenue, or of some sudden forced extortion of a war indemnity or other public penalty. It is a direct object of imperialist finance to create other debts, just as it is an object of the private money-lender to goad his clients into pecuniary difficulties in order that they may have recourse to him" (Hobson [1905] 1972, 108). More specifically:

> The direct military and naval expenditure during the period has increased faster than the total expenditure, the growth of trade, of national income, or any other general indication of national resources. In 1875 the army and navy cost less than 24.5 millions out of a total expenditure of 65 millions; in 1903 they cost nearly 79 millions out of a total of 140 millions. . . .
>
> This growth of naval and military expenditure from about 25 to 79 millions in little over a quarter of a century is the most significant fact of imperialist finance. The financial, industrial and professional classes, who, we have shown, form the economic core of Imperialism, have used their political power to extract these sums from the nation in order to improve their investments and open up new fields for capital, and to find profitable markets for their surplus goods, while out of the public sums expended on these objects they reap other great profitable gains in the shape of profitable contracts and lucrative or honorable employment.
>
> The financial and industrial capitalists who have mainly engineered this policy, employing their ill-recognized business ends, have also made important bribes or concessions to other less directly benefitted interest in order to keep their sympathy and ensure their support. . . .
>
> The economic cost of militarism is therefore twofold; the greatly increased expense of the army must be defrayed by an impoverished people. (95–96, 133)

But would the people of Britain stand for a policy that pushes for a constantly growing public debt, increasing militarization, and a long-run decline in the standard of living in the nation? Would they be willing to finance such a policy had they been told of its actual dynamics? "Were the capitalist-imperialist forces openly to shift the burden of taxation on to the shoulders of the people," replied Hobson, "it would be difficult under popular forms of government to operate such an expensive policy. The people must pay, but they must not know they are paying, or how much they are paying, and the payment must be spread over as long a period as possible" (98).

Hobson's detailed observations on the nature, causes, and manifestations of modern imperialism led him to the following inescapable conclusion:

> Our economic analysis has disclosed the fact that it is only the interests of competing cliques of businessmen—investors, contractors, export manufacturers, and certain professional classes—that are antagonistic; that these cliques, usurping the authority and voice of the people, use the public resources to push their private interests, and spend the blood and money of the people in this vast and disastrous military game, feigning national antagonisms which have no basis in reality. It is not to the interest of the British people, either as producers of wealth or as taxpayers, to risk a war . . . but it may serve the interest of a group of commercial politicians to promote this dangerous policy. . . .
>
> War, however, represents not the success, but the failure of this policy; its normal and most perilous fruit is not war, but militarism: So long as this competitive expansion for territory and foreign markets is permitted to misrepresent itself as "national policy" the antagonism of interests seems real, and the people seat and bleed and toil to keep up an evermore expensive machinery of war. ([1905] 1972, 127–128)

As real as the economic manifestations and political-military implications of modern British imperialism were, and although Hobson did not deny the immense power of these economic factors, he nonetheless did not view imperialism as the necessary outcome of capitalist development. Hobson readily admitted that the conditions of contemporary capitalism constitute the "taproot of imperialism," but he denied that these conditions were unavoidable. Contrary to the argument later developed by Lenin, Hobson repeatedly acknowledged that capitalism would indeed survive and prosper without imperialism. To Hobson imperialism was a disease, a disease inflicted on an otherwise healthy body (capitalism). Thus, in order for capitalism to prosper, imperialism—which cost the people immense amounts that were wasted in the process of unnecessary militarization—was to be eliminated. And this change could come, thought Hobson, through political pressure by the taxpayers that would lead to the needed reforms.

There were no reasons in Hobson's mind that would indicate the necessity of imperialism. To dispel the notion of "necessity," as was advanced by the imperialist sympathizers of the period, Hobson pointed out time and again that the driving force behind imperialism is a definite class interest and to eliminate imperialism "the axe [must be] laid at the economic root of the tree" and, in this way, the elimination of the special privileges of the classes for whose interests imperialism works. Since Hobson did not see an inevitable link between imperialism and capitalism, he believed that the "economic root" could be cut even while capitalism prevailed.

> If the consuming public in this country raised its standard of consumption to keep pace with every rise of productive powers, there could be no excess of goods or capital clamorous to use Imperialism in order to find markets; foreign trade would indeed exist, but there would be no difficulty in exchanging a small surplus of our manufactures for the food and raw material we annually absorbed, and all the savings that we made could find employment, if we choose, in home industries. ([1905] 1972, 81)

What Hobson suggested, then, is quite clear; he advocated the abolition of imperialism, the breakup of monopolies, and the return to competitive, laissez-faire capitalism.

THE MARXIST FORMULATION OF THE PROBLEM: LUXEMBURG AND LENIN

The conclusions reached by Hobson on the question of the "necessity of imperialism," place him in direct opposition to the analyses developed by Luxemburg and Lenin.

Luxemburg's Contribution

Luxemburg, unlike Hobson, developed a systematic argument for the economic necessity of imperialism. According to Luxemburg, the expansion of capitalism to the peripheral regions of the world capitalist system was a manifestation of the inherently expansionary nature of capital accumulation. The integration of new consumers previously outside the capitalist market relations into the world capitalist system was the sine qua non of capital accumulation. This point is made quite clear by Luxemburg:

> [C]apitalist production does not aim at its products being enjoyed, but at the accumulation of surplus value. There had been no demand for the surplus product within the country so capital had lain idle without the possibility of accumulating. But abroad, where capitalist production has not yet developed, there has come about, voluntarily or by force, a new demand for the non-capitalist strata. . . . The important point is that capital accumulated in the old country should find elsewhere new opportunities to beget and realize surplus value so that accumulation can proceed. In the new countries, large regions of natural economy

are open to conversion into commodity economy or exiting commodity economy can be ousted by capital. ([1913] 1951, 427–428)

She maintained that a closed capitalist system in the face of monopolization of the market was impossible. Thus, the capitalist system, she argued,
was rapidly expanding to all corners of the world in order to integrate areas
that had previously remained untapped by capitalists, "Enlarged reproduction, i.e., accumulation is possible only if new districts with a non-capitalist
civilization, extending over large areas, appear on the scene and augment the
number of consumers" ([1913] 1951, 429). This, in essence, was Luxemburg's central thesis on the theory of imperialism, "Imperialism is the political expression of the accumulation of capital in its competitive struggle for
what remains still open of the non-capitalist environment" (446). She argued:

> Still the largest part of the world in terms of geography, this remaining field for
> the expansion of capital is yet insignificant as against the high level of develop-
> ment already attained by the productive forces of capital; witness the immense
> masses of capital accumulated in the old countries which seek an outlet for their
> surplus product and strive to capitalize their surplus value and the rapid change-
> over to capitalism of the pre-capitalist civilizations. On the international stage,
> then, capital must take appropriate measures. With the high development of the
> capitalist countries and their increasingly severe competition in acquiring non-
> capitalist areas, imperialism grows in lawlessness and violence, both in aggres-
> sion against the non-capitalist countries. But the more violently, ruthlessly and
> throughly imperialism brings about the decline of non-capitalist civilizations,
> the more rapidly it cuts the very ground from under the feet of capitalist accu-
> mulation. Though imperialism is the historical method for prolonging the career
> of capitalism, it is also a sure means of bringing it to a swift conclusion. This is
> not to say that capitalist development must be actually driven to this extreme:
> the mere tendency toward imperialism of itself takes forms which make the fi-
> nal phase of capitalism a period of catastrophe. (446)

The expansion of capital into the peripheral regions of the world and their
integration into the world capitalist system convinced Luxemburg of the existence of a mechanism through which that expansion could take place. This
mechanism, tied to the export of capital to precapitalist regions, was none
other than the large overseas loans advanced by the big financial houses of
Western capitalist centers. To illustrate this clearly, she wrote, "For the accumulation of capital the loan has various functions . . . it serves to divert accumulated capital from the old capitalist countries to young ones" ([1913]
1951, 420). More specifically, "In the sixteenth and seventeenth centuries, the
loan transferred capital from the Italian cities to England, in the eighteenth

century from Holland to England, in the nineteenth century from England to the American Republics and Australia, from France, Germany and Belgium to Russia, and at the present time [1912] from Germany to Turkey, from England, Germany and France to China and via Russia, to Persia" (420–421).

While the transfer of capital continued to flow from the advanced to the previously undeveloped countries of the world capitalist system, herein lay the contradiction of the system on a global scale: To expand the capitalist market, hence the process of capital accumulation, globally, capital is extended to previously noncapitalist regions; by doing this, through foreign loans "the old capitalist states maintain their influence, exercise financial control and exert pressure on the customs, foreign and commercial policy of the capitalist states"; and in this way, it creates the conditions for its downfall at the widest possible level of worldwide economic crises and political and social turmoil (Luxemburg [1913] 1951, 421). As Luxemburg showed throughout her study, "its movement of accumulation provides a solution to the conflict and aggravates it at the same time" (467). Thus, "the more ruthlessly capital sets about the destruction of non-capitalist strata at home and in the outside world," she concludes, "the more it lowers the standard of living for the workers as a whole, the greater also is the change in the day-to-day history of capital. It becomes a string of political and social disasters and political convulsions, and under these conditions, punctuated by periodical economic catastrophes or crises, accumulation can go on no longer" (466–467).

In the closing pages of her book, Luxemburg gives us a brief summary of the accumulation process of the capitalist mode of production, linking it to its new, international stage, which has extended the base of capital accumulation from the national to the global level:

> Thus capital accumulation as a whole, as an actual historical process, has two different aspects. One concerns the commodity market and the place where surplus value is produced—the factory, the mine, the agricultural estate. Regarded in this light, accumulation is a purely economic process, with its most important phase a transaction between the capitalist and wage laborer. . . .
>
> The other aspect of the accumulation of capital concerns the relations between capitalism and the non-capitalist modes of production which start making their appearance on the international stage. Its predominant methods are colonial policy, an international loan system—a policy of spheres of interest—and war. Force, fraud, oppression, looting are openly displayed without any attempt at concealment, and it requires an effort to discover within this tangle of political violence and contests of power the stern laws of the economic process. . . .
>
> In reality, political power is nothing but a vehicle for the economic process. The condition for the reproduction of capital provides the organic link between

these two aspects of the accumulation of capital. The historical career of capitalism can only be appreciated by taking them together. "Sweating blood and filth with every pore from head to toe" characterizes not only the birth of capital but also its progress in the world at every step, and thus capitalism prepares its own downfall under ever more violent contortions and convulsions. ([1913] 1951, 452–453)

Lenin's Theory

Lenin's theory of imperialism centered essentially around the five fundamental features of the highest stage of capitalist development:

1. The concentration of production and capital has developed to such a high stage that it has created monopolies that play a decisive role in economic life
2. Bank capital has merged with industrial capital and created, on the basis of this "finance capital," a financial oligarchy
3. The export of commodities acquires exceptional importance
4. International monopolist capitalist combines form and share the world among themselves
5. The territorial division of the whole world among the biggest capitalist powers is completed

The beginning point of Lenin's analysis of imperialism is his conception of the dynamics of modern capitalism: the concentration and monopolization of production, "The enormous growth of industry and the remarkably rapid concentration of production in ever larger enterprises are one of the most characteristic features of capitalism. . . . [A]t a certain stage of its development concentration itself, as it were, leads straight to monopoly, for a score or so of giant enterprises can easily arrive at an agreement" to monopolize the market ([1917] 1975, 642, 643). He argued that "[t]his transformation of competition into monopoly is one of the most important—if not the most important— phenomena of modern capitalist economy" (643). Referring to Karl Marx's *Das Capital,* Lenin pointed out that "by a theoretical and historical analysis of capitalism [Marx] proved that free competition gives rise to the concentration of production, which, in turn, at a certain stage of development, leads to monopoly" (645). "Today," he adds, "monopoly has become a fact . . . and that the rise of monopolies, as a result of the concentration of production, is a general and fundamental law of the present stage of development of capitalism" (645). In outlining the dynamics of competitive capitalism developing into its special, monopoly stage (i.e., imperialism), Lenin noted that the principal stages in the history of monopolies are the following: (1) 1860–70, the highest stage, the apex of development of free competition; monopoly is in the barely discernible, embryonic stage; (2) After the crisis of 1873, a lengthy period of development of cartels; but they are still the exception. They are not yet durable. They are still a transitory phenomenon; (3) The boom at the end of the nineteenth century and the crisis of 1900–03. Cartels became one of the foundations of the whole of economic life. Capitalism has been transformed into imperialism. (646–647)

He observed that:

Cartels come to an agreement on the terms of sale, dates of payment, etc. They divide the markets among themselves. They fix the quantity of goods to be produced. They fix prices. They divide the profits among the various enterprises, etc. . . . In order to prevent competition . . . the monopolists even resort to various stratagems: they spread false rumors about the bad situation in their industry; anonymous warnings are published in the newspapers; lastly, they buy up "outsiders" (those outside the syndicates) and pay them "compensation." (647, 651–652)

For Lenin, "the real power and significance of modern monopolies" could not be understood unless one took "into consideration the part played by the banks" ([1917] 1975, 653).

The principal and primary functions of banks is to serve as middlemen in the making of payments. . . .
   As banking develops and becomes concentrated in a small number of establishments, the banks grow from modest middlemen into powerful monopolies. . . . This transformation of numerous modest middlemen into a handful of monopolists is one of the fundamental processes in the growth of capitalism into capitalist imperialism. (653)

After examining an enormous quantity of data, Lenin came to the following conclusions on the concentration of banking, especially in Germany, and the extent to which banks control the market and the significance of that control:

The small banks are being squeezed out by the big banks, of which only nine concentrate in their hands almost half the total deposits. . . . The big enterprises, and the banks in particular, not only completely absorb the small ones, but also "annex" them, subordinate them, bring them into their "own" group or "concern" (to use the technical term) by acquiring "holdings" in their capital, by purchasing or exchanging shares, by a system of credits, etc., etc. . . .

We see the rapid expansion of a close network of channels which cover the whole country, centralizing all capital and all revenues, transforming thousands and thousands of scattered economic enterprises into a single national capitalist, and then into a world capitalist economy. . . .

. . . [T]he concentration of capital and the growth of bank turnover are radically changing the significance of the banks. Scattered capitalists are transformed into a single collective capitalist. When carrying the current accounts of a few capitalists, a bank, as it were, transacts a purely technical and exclusively auxiliary operation. When, however, this operation grows to enormous dimensions we find that a handful of monopolists subordinate to their will all the operations, both commercial and industrial, of the whole of capitalist society; for they are enabled—by means of their banking connections, their current accounts and other financial operations—first, to *ascertain exactly* the financial position of the various capitalist, then to *control* them, to influence them by restricting or enlarging, facilitating or hindering credits, and finally *entirely determine* their fate. . . .

Among the few banks which remain at the head of all capitalist economy as a result of the process of concentration, there is naturally to be observed an increasingly marked tendency towards monopolist agreements, towards a *bank trust*. . . .

Again and again the final work in the development of banking is monopoly. ([1917] 1975, 654–662)

Lenin's detailed study of the process of concentration and monopolization of banking in the major capitalist countries at the turn of the twentieth century convinced him to conclude that, "at all events, in all capitalist countries, notwithstanding all the differences in their banking laws, banks greatly intensify and accelerate the process of concentration of capital and the formation of monopolies" ([1917] 1975, 658). Lenin then explained the "close connection between the banks and industry." The monopolistic relationship between the banks and industrial capitalists is such that "the industrial capitalist becomes more completely dependent on the bank" (662). To stress the existence of this mutual relationship and to outline the specific mechanisms through which such a relationship is established, Lenin pointed out that "a personal union, so to speak, is established between the banks and the biggest industrial and commercial enterprises, the merging of one with another through the acquisition of shares, through the appointment of bank directors to the Supervisory Boards (or Boards of Directors) of industrial and commercial enterprises, and vice versa" (662).

All of these, then, signify to Lenin (1) "the ever-growing merger of bank and industrial capital" and (2) "the growth of the banks into institutions of a truly 'universal character'" (Lenin [1917] 1975, 664). "Thus, the twentieth century marks the turning point from the old capitalism to the new, from the domination of capital in general to the domination of finance capital" (666).

In his chapter on finance capital and the financial oligarchy, Lenin, by way of quoting Rudolf Hilferding, clarified the underlying dynamics of "finance capital." According to Hilferding, "bank capital, i.e., capital in money form, which is . . . transformed into industrial capital," can be called "finance capital." In other words, "finance capital is capital controlled by banks and employed by industrialists" (Hilferding, as quoted in Lenin [1917] 1975, 667). But, to Lenin, "this definition is incomplete insofar as it is silent on one extremely important fact": "[T]he increase of concentration of production and of capital to such an extent that concentration is leading, and has led, to monopoly. . . . The concentration of production; the monopolies arising therefrom; the merging or coalescence of the banks with industry—such is the history of the rise of finance capital and such is the content of that concept" (667).

Lenin then described "how, under the general conditions of commodity production and private property, the 'business operations' of capitalist monopolies inevitably lead to the domination of a financial oligarchy" ([1917] 1975, 667). And the "cornerstone" of that domination is the "holding system." (As an example of this, Lenin mentioned the Deutsche Bank "group" as "one of the biggest, if not the biggest, of the big banking groups.") Quoting from the work of the German economist Hans Gidion Heymann, Lenin developed the following observations of the nature and structure of the "holding system":

> The head of the concern controls the principal company (literally: the "mother company"); the latter reigns over the subsidiary companies ("daughter companies") which in their turn control still other subsidiaries ("grandchild companies"), etc. In this way, it is possible with a comparatively small capital to dominate immense spheres of production. Indeed, if holding 50 percent of the capital is always sufficient to control a company, the head of the concern needs only one million to control eight million in the second subsidiaries. And if this "interlocking" is extended, it is possible with one million to control sixteen million, thirty-two million, etc. (Heymann, as quoted in Lenin [1917] 1975, 668)

Basing his facts on bourgeois sources, such as Professor Robert Liefman (an "apologist of imperialism and of finance capital"), Lenin argued that "it is sufficient to own 40 per cent of the shares of a company in order to direct its affairs" (668). The "holding system," he added, "not only serves enormously to increase the power of the monopolists; it also enables them to resort with impunity to all sorts of shady and dirty tricks to cheat the public, for the directors of the 'mother company' are not legally responsible for the 'daughter company,' which is supposed to be 'independent,' and *through the medium* of which they can 'pull off' *anything"* (669). And to illustrate his point, Lenin cited several examples from the publications of finance capital itself (e.g., *Die Bank*).

In short, finance capital

> concentrated in a few hands and exercising a virtual monopoly, exacts enormous and ever-increasing profits from the floating of companies, issue of stock, state loans, etc., strengthens the domination of the financial oligarchy and levies tribute upon the whole of society for the benefit of monopolists. . . . The supremacy of finance capital over all other forms of capital means the predominance of the rentier and of the financial oligarchy; it means that a small number of financially "powerful" states stand out among all the rest. (Lenin [1917] 1975, 672, 677)

And these states, made up of "the richest capitalist countries" (England, the United States, France, and Germany), together "own 479,000,000,000 francs, that is, nearly 80 per cent of the world's finance capital" (678). "In one way or another," Lenin added, "nearly the whole of the rest of the world is more or less the debtor to and tributary of these international banker countries, these four 'pillars' of world finance capital" (678).

The obvious international implications of world finance capital led Lenin to examine next the part that the export of capital plays in creating the international network of dependence and connections of finance capital. He argued that unlike under conditions of competition when the principal characteristic of capitalism is the export of *goods,* under the rule of monopolies, it is the export of *capital:*

> On the threshold of the twentieth century we see the formation of a new type of monopoly: firstly, monopolist associations of capitalists in all capitalistically developed countries; secondly, the monopolist position of a few very rich countries, in which the accumulation of capital has reached gigantic proportions. An enormous "surplus of capital" has arisen in the advanced countries.
> . . . As long as capitalism remains what it is, surplus capital will be utilized not for the purpose of raising the standard of living of the masses in a given country, for this would mean a decline of profits for the capitalists, but for the purpose of increasing profits by exporting capital abroad to the backward countries. In these backward countries profits are usually high, for capital is scarce, the price of land is relatively low, wages are low, raw materials are cheap. The export of capital is made possible by a number of backward countries having already been drawn into world capitalist intercourse; main railways have either been or are being built in those countries, elementary conditions for industrial

development have been created, etc. The need to export capital arises from the fact that in a few countries capitalism has become "overripe" and (owing to the backward state of agriculture and the poverty of the masses) capital cannot find a field for "profitable" investment. . . .

The export of capital influences and greatly accelerates the development of capitalism in those countries to which it is exported. While, therefore, the export of capital may tend to a certain extent to arrest development in the capital-exporting countries, it can only do so by expanding and deepening the further development of capitalism throughout the world. ([1917] 1975, 679, 681)

An important channel through which capital is exported to the peripheral countries is international loans. Quoting from an article in *Die Bank,* Lenin pointed out that, in making these loans, the capital-exporting countries are nearly always able to obtain "advantages": "In these international transactions the creditor nearly always manages to secure some extra benefit: a favorable clause in a commercial treaty, a coaling station, a contract, a harbor, a fat concession, or an order for guns" ([1917] 1975, 681). "The most usual thing" in this financial transaction "is to stipulate that part of the loan that is granted shall be spent on purchases in the creditor country, particularly on orders for war materials, or for ships, etc. . . . The export of capital thus becomes a means for encouraging the export of commodities" (681). All these observations led Lenin to conclude that "the capital-exporting countries have divided the world among themselves in the figurative sense of the term. But finance capital has led to the *actual* division of the world" (683).

Lenin argued that the economic division of the world among capitalist combines was the inherent outcome of the development of capitalism into its highest stage: monopoly capital.

Monopolist capitalist combines, cartels, syndicates and trusts first divided the home market among themselves and obtained more or less complete possession of the industry of their own country. But under capitalism the home market is inevitably bound up with the foreign market. Capitalism long ago created a world market. As the export of capital increased, and as the foreign and colonial connections and "spheres of influence" of the big monopolist combines expanded in all ways, things "naturally" gravitated towards an international agreement among these combines, and towards the formation of international cartels.

This is a new stage of world concentration of capital and production, incomparably higher than the preceding stages. ([1917] 1975, 683)

To illustrate how this "supermonopoly" develops, Lenin examined the electric industry, which, he said, is "highly typical of the latest technical achievements and is most typical of capitalism at the *end* of the nineteenth and the beginning of the twentieth centuries" ([1917] 1975, 683). Drawing attention to the monopolization of this sector of global industrial capital, he noted that "this industry has developed most in the two leaders of the new capitalist countries, the United States and Germany" (683). After examining the process of a series of mergers in the global electrical industry from 1900 to 1912, he concluded that "*two* electrical 'great powers' were formed":

> [I]n 1907, the German and American trust concluded an agreement by which they divided the world between them. Competition between them ceased. The American General Electric Company (G.E.C.) "got" the United States and Canada. The German General Electric Company (A.E.G.) "got" Germany, Austria, Russia, Holland, Denmark, Switzerland, Turkey and the Balkans. Special agreements, naturally secret, were concluded regarding the penetration of "daughter companies" into new branches of industry, into "new" countries formally not yet allotted. The two trusts were to exchange inventions and experiments. (685)

But for Lenin, such agreements to divide the world are only temporary and do not "preclude *redivision* if the relation of forces changes as a result of uneven development, war, bankruptcy, etc." ([1917] 1975, 685). And to support his argument, he cited the fierce struggle for redivision then taking place in the international oil industry: a struggle between John D. Rockefeller's Standard Oil Company and the big German banks, headed by the giant Deutsche Bank, for the controlling interests of the oil industry in Romania, "On the one hand, the Rockefeller 'oil trust' wanted to lay its hands on *everything;* it formed a 'daughter company' *right* in Holland, and bought up oil fields in the Dutch Indies, in order to strike at its principal enemy, the Anglo-Dutch Shell trust. On the other hand, the Deutsche bank and the other German banks aimed at 'retaining' Romania 'for themselves' and at uniting her with Russia against Rockefeller" (686).

The conclusion Lenin reached was thus inescapable: The division and redivision of the world is the result of a permanent struggle between two or more major capitalist powers, for this is the essence of the contradiction within international monopoly capital (interimperialist rivalry):

> The capitalists divide the world, not out of any particular malice, but because the degree of concentration which has been reached forces them to adopt this method in order to obtain profits. And they divide it "in proportion to capital," "in proportion to strength." . . . But strength varies with the degree of economic and political development. In order to understand what is taking place, it is necessary to know what questions are settled by the changes in strength. ([1917] 1975, 689)

Moreover, "the epoch of the latest stage of capitalism shows us that certain relations between capitalist combines grow up, *based on* the economic division of the world; while parallel to and in connection with it, certain relations grow up between political alliances, between states, on the basis of the territorial division of the world, of the struggle for colonies, of the 'struggle for spheres of influence'" (689–690).

Thus, the characteristic feature of the epoch of the international expansion of monopoly capital, Lenin argued, is the final and definitive partition of the world—final, in the sense that repartition in the future is possible only in the form of transferring territories from one "owner" to another. This is so because "the colonial policy of the capitalist countries has *completed* the seizure of the unoccupied territories on our planet. For the first time the world is completely divided up" (Lenin [1917] 1975, 690). Related to this territorial division of the world, Lenin hinted at the existence of yet another motive force behind imperialism. He argued that as capitalism develops, the need for raw materials (essential for the continued reproduction of capital) increases, and this intensifies the competition between rival imperialist powers to acquire the sources of these raw materials throughout the world. This international rivalry in turn leads the imperialist countries to pursue imperial policies. This is summarized by Lenin in an important passage in *Imperialism,* "The more capitalism is developed, the more strongly the shortage of raw materials is felt, the more intense the competition and the hunt for sources of raw materials throughout the whole world, the more desperate the struggle for the acquisition of colonies" (695).

Thus, as the principal feature of imperialism is domination by giant monopolies of advanced capitalist countries, "these monopolies are most firmly established," argued Lenin, "when *all* the sources of raw materials are captured by one group. . . . Colonial possession alone gives the monopolies complete guarantee against all contingencies in the struggle against competitors" ([1917] 1975, 695).

Finally, with regard to colonial policy "in the epoch of capitalist imperialism," Lenin observed that "finance capital and its foreign policy, which is the struggle of the great powers for the economic and political division of the world, give rise to a number of *transitional* forms of state dependence" ([1917] 1975, 697). Typical of this epoch is not only the group of countries that own colonies, and the colonies themselves, "but also the diverse forms of dependent countries which politically are formally independent, but in fact, are enmeshed in the net of financial and diplomatic dependence" (697). These relations of dependence between the dominant and dependent states "in the epoch of capitalist imperialism become a general system . . . become links in the chain of operations of world finance capital" (698).

There are two other important points that Lenin raised: the parasitism of imperialism and, its consequence, the bourgeoisification of certain segments among the workers in the imperialist countries. Lenin maintained that the "superexploitation" of the colonies by the advanced capitalist countries has resulted in the latter turning from "productive" to "parasitic" states:

> Imperialism is an immense accumulation of money capital in a few countries. . . . Hence the extraordinary growth of a class, or rather, of a stratum of rentiers, i.e., people who live by "clipping coupons," who take no part in any enterprise whatever, whose profession is idleness. The export of capital, one of the most essential economic bases of imperialism, still more completely isolates the rentiers from production and sets the seal of parasitism on the whole country that lives by exploiting the labor of several overseas countries and colonies. . . .
>
> Monopolies, oligarchy, the striving for domination, . . . the exploitation of an increasing number of small or weak nations by a handful of the richest or most powerful nations—all these have given birth to those distinctive characteristics of imperialism which compel us to define it as parasitic or decaying capitalism. ([1917] 1975, 709–710)

Furthermore, the receipt of enormous monopoly profits by the imperialist bourgeoisie "makes it economically possible for them to bribe certain sections of the workers . . . and win them to the side of the bourgeoisie of a given industry or given nation against all the others" (728).

The underlying argument of Lenin's analysis of imperialism as the highest stage of capitalism is that imperialism is the *necessary* outcome of the development of capitalism:

> Imperialism emerged as the development and direct continuation of the fundamental characteristics of capitalism in general. But capitalism only became capitalist imperialism at a definite and very high stage of its development. . . . Economically, the main thing in this process is the displacement of capitalist free competition by capitalist monopoly. . . . Monopoly is the transition from capitalism to a higher system.
>
> If it were necessary to give the briefest possible definition of imperialism we should have to say that imperialism is the monopoly stage of capitalism. ([1917] 1975, 699–700)

Thus, in summarizing the fundamental features of imperialism, Lenin concluded, "Imperialism is capitalism in that stage of development in which the dominance of monopolies and finance capital is established; in which the export of capital has acquired pronounced importance; in which the division of world among the international trusts has begun; in which the division of all territories of the globe among the biggest capitalist powers has been completed" ([1917] 1975, 700).

THE POLITICAL IMPLICATIONS
OF THE VARIOUS POSITIONS

We have seen that there are certain similarities in the positions advanced by Hobson, Luxemburg, and Lenin. They all argued that modern imperialism is a manifestation of the interests of the dominant classes in a handful of developed capitalist countries and that it is beneficial to a section of the capitalist class engaged in overseas investment and finance as well as to other sections of the bourgeoisie that are linked to it. They also agreed that economic gain, derived from the international operations of the big bourgeoisie (and the safeguarding of such operations on a world scale), constitutes the motive force of imperialism. Thus, the accumulation of capital and its appropriation by the capitalist class at the world level (through the mechanisms of the capitalist state, which this class controls) lies at the heart of the process of international capitalist expansion, hence of imperialism. But this is where the similarities end.

Hobson, who gave us the clues of the link between monopoly capital at home and its operations overseas as the basis of imperialism, nonetheless failed to recognize that modern imperialism (or monopoly capital operating on a global scale) is the direct and inevitable outcome of the development of capitalism itself. This failure to understand the very dynamics of capitalism and the origins of imperialist finance capital led him to view imperialism as an "unnecessary *policy*" of the trusts, which can be eliminated without affecting capitalism. Failing to develop a thorough class analysis of Britain (the social formation under study), he viewed the problem (imperialism) from the angle of "the nation" as a whole. This liberal "error," however, was well in line with Hobson's social-democratic conception of capitalism. That is, he had no qualms about capitalism as such, but only about some of its undesirable manifestations, that is, imperialism, that led to global wars, oppression of colonial and semicolonial peoples, and so on. This meant a larger public debt and increased taxes to be paid by the people. Viewed within this framework, Hobson's only recourse was to convince the monopolists (and their politicians in the Parliament) that in the long run it would be more profitable for them to confine themselves to the national market, for the problem of overproduction/underconsumption could be overcome simply by raising wages, which would expand the purchasing power of the workers and lead to an increase in local consumption. How Hobson thought the monopolists would raise wages (which in fact would lower profits) and agree to the relinquishment of their global investments of future profitability based on expanded national consumption is a puzzle that only idealists such as Hobson could dream up. Notwithstanding his wish to return to the old days of laissez-faire, his only counsel to the masses was to put pressure on the Parliament and, if necessary, boycott taxes in order to block the assistance of the state to the monopolists. These are the implications of Hobson's reformist politics on imperialism that are rooted in his conception of the relationship of imperialism to capitalism and in his nonproletarian, petit bourgeois/populist view of the contradictions of the highest stage of capitalist economics.

Luxemburg's and Lenin's arguments are similar and complementary to each other, although they contain some notable variations in emphasis. Luxemburg's argument largely rested on the crisis of overproduction and the necessity of the export of goods (and later capital) for the continued accumulation of capital. Hence, this necessity, which is built into the capitalist system (given that wages are always at a much lower level than that required for the purchase of all the commodities produced), forces the capitalists to realize profit through expansion to colonial and semicolonial areas that fall outside of capitalist market relations (as well as through the domination of those that are already part of the world economy). Through the state, which facilitates the expansionary process by extending loans and "aid" to these areas, the capitalists are able to dump their surplus goods and realize profit. Such profit is then invested in the colonies and semicolonies to further expand the accumulation process and with it the exploitation of labor at global proportions.

Lenin's argument stressed the domination of the export of capital over the export of goods in this period. His emphasis on the importance of the export of capital is crucial from the angle of its implications concerning the transformation of the relations of production in the colonial and semicolonial areas. With the export of capital, and the employment of wage-labor that this capital requires in the periphery, Lenin saw that capitalism had reached its highest and final stage and that as a result exploited workers throughout the world will rise up in arms against it. Hence, his conclusion in the preface to *Imperialism,* "Imperialism is the eve of the social revolution of the proletariat . . . on a world wide scale" ([1917] 1975, 640).

While the implications of Luxemburg's conclusions are similar to those of Lenin's on the question of the exploitation of labor at the global level and the inevitable consequences of this conflict between the exploiter and exploited that will result in proletarian revolution throughout the world, Luxemburg nonetheless placed more of an emphasis on the narrow economic consequences of capitalism, the central one of which is the crisis of overproduction, now at global (and more catastrophic) proportions. It is this economic crisis preventing more and more the further realization of profit that will bring the downfall of world capitalism, according to Luxemburg. And it is in this sense that Luxemburg ended up developing a "crisis theory" of capitalism as opposed to its revolutionary overthrow by the politically organized international proletariat—a conclusion to be drawn in its clearest form from the arguments presented by Lenin.

Chapter Three

The Controversy over Globalization, Imperialism, and Capitalist Development on a World Scale

The rapid expansion of capitalism throughout the world during the latter half of the twentieth century and the accelerated spread of capitalist relations of production on a worldwide basis during this period has led to the proliferation of literature and renewed discussion and debate on globalization, imperialism, and capitalist development on a world scale (see El-bakidze 2002).

Much of the controversy on globalization has been over its seemingly unique features, and for this reason some have characterized it as a qualitatively *new stage* of capitalism and capitalist development. Critics of this view, however, have argued in favor of an alternative position that situates contemporary global capitalism within the context of the development of modern imperialism (see Petras and Veltmeyer 2001). Globalization, viewed in this way, can be seen as the engine of capitalist expansion on a global scale, and as such facilitating the accumulation of capital throughout the world.

The globalization of capital, then, can be viewed as a process of imperialist expansion that leads to capitalist development in the less developed regions of the world.[1] Whatever form this development may take, the arguments presented in favor of this view, I argue, are contrary to that of the dependency/world-system approach that dominated development studies during the past three decades. Adopting an alternative Marxist approach, I provide a critical analysis of the globalization of capital and capitalist development from the standpoint of the Marxist theory of imperialism as articulated by V. I. Lenin.

47

THEORETICAL CONSIDERATIONS

The theoretical approach countering globalization presented in recent Marxist works is not an entirely new interpretation of the classical Marxist theory of colonialism, imperialism, and capital accumulation on a world scale that has dominated the debate among Marxist circles for more than a century. In writing about the East India Company in 1853, Karl Marx saw Britain as fulfilling "a double mission in India: one destructive, the other regenerating" ([1853] 1986, 46). He projected that the "means of irrigation and of internal communication," "the immediate and current wants of railway locomotion" could be the "forerunner of modern industry" (47–49). Referring to the impact of British rule on Indian villages, "however much the English may have hibernicized the country," Marx wrote in a letter to Friedrich Engels, "the breaking up of those stereotyped primitive forms was the *sine qua non* for Europeanization. The tax-gatherer alone could not achieve this. The destruction of their ancient industry was necessary to deprive the villages of their self-supporting character" (192).

Lenin, in his classic work *Imperialism: The Highest Stage of Capitalism,* wrote, "The export of capital influences and greatly accelerates the development of capitalism in those countries to which it is exported. While, therefore, the export of capital may tend to a certain extent to arrest development in the capital-exporting countries, it can only do so by expanding and deepening the further development of capitalism throughout the world" ([1917] 1975, 681). Thus, "capitalism is growing with the greatest rapidity in the colonies and in overseas countries" (707).

Marx and Lenin were interested in the contradictions of this capitalist expansionary process above all from the angle of the proletariat and the laboring masses in the colonies and in the colonial centers. "All the English bourgeoisie may be forced to do," Marx wrote in *The Future Results of the British Rule in India,* "will neither emancipate nor materially mend the social condition of the mass of the people [in India]. . . . But what they will not fail to do is to lay down the material premises for both. Has the bourgeoisie ever done more? Has it ever effected a progress without dragging individuals and peoples through blood and dirt, through misery and degradation?" ([1853] 1986, 50). He added, "The Indians will not reap the fruits of the new elements of society scattered among them by the British bourgeoisie, till in Great Britain itself the now ruling classes shall have been supplanted by the industrial proletariat, or till the Hindus themselves shall have grown strong enough to throw off the English yoke altogether" (50).

These concerns are also expressed by Lenin in his book *Imperialism:*

> The building of railways seems to be a simple, natural, democratic, cultural and civilizing enterprise; that is what it is in the opinion of bourgeois professors who are paid to depict capitalist slavery in bright colors, and in the opinion of petty-bourgeois philistines. But as a matter of fact the capitalist threads, which in the thousands of different intercrossings bind these enterprises with private property in means of production in general, have converted this railway construction into an instrument of oppressing *a thousand million* people (in the colonies and semi-colonies), that is, more than half the population of the globe that inhabits the dependent countries, as well as the wage-slaves of capital in the "civilized" countries. ([1917] 1975, 637)

Further on, Lenin explained:

> The description of "British imperialism" in Schulze-Gaevermitz's book reveals the same parasitical traits. . . . While the "merit" of imperialism is that it "trains the Negro to habits of industry" (not without coercion, of course . . .), the "danger" of imperialism lies in that "Europe will shift the burden of physical toil— first agricultural and mining, then the rougher work in industry—on to the colored races, and itself be content with the role of rentier, and in this way, perhaps, pave the way for the economic, and later, the political emancipation of the colored races." ([1917] 1975, 712–713)

Thus, Lenin concluded, "Imperialism is the eve of the social revolution of the proletariat . . . on a world wide scale" (640).

In the light of the previous observations by Marx and Lenin, I would argue that recent Marxist works critical of globalization are firmly rooted in the classical Marxist theory of capitalist imperialism. And this stands in sharp contrast to the dependency/world-system approach that has dominated development studies for three decades.

While both world-system theory and Marxism contend that they offer a concrete analysis of the capitalist political economy on a global level, I would argue that in fact only the latter offers us a coherent explanation through the formulation of the problem in terms of the laws of motion of the capitalist mode of production in its global manifestations.

For world-system theory, the basic units of analysis are "nation-states" and the "world system," and "exploitation" takes place between these units at the level of circulation, resulting in "unequal exchange" (effected through "core-periphery" relations of domination). Marxism, however, argues that in studying development one must always start with an analysis of social classes and class relations (at both national and international levels) and that the focus of analysis should be the exploitation of labor rooted in relations of production in specific social formations.[2]

As we shall see shortly, the political implications of the two sets of theories vary sharply when we view the question of imperialist expansion in these divergent terms. Thus, while the advocates of world-system theory argue that imperialism "blocks" capitalist development in the Third World and that therefore the dominated countries ought to "break away from the world system,"[3] Marxists concentrate directly on the relations of production under imperialism and focus on the class nature of imperialist exploitation, moving beyond national/institutional issues such as unequal trade, foreign debt, and technological dependence, to a characterization of imperialism as an extended form of the capitalist mode of appropriation of surplus value from workers on a world scale (Szymanski 1981; Berberoglu 1987b).

Not grounded in an analysis of the laws of motion of capitalism originating in the imperial centers and its subsequent expansion through various stages to the economically backward areas of the Third World, world-system theory starts from the subjective-empiricist notion that globalization exists in a vacuum and defines development in subjective terms. Thus, while this particular conceptualization of imperialism is a major shortcoming of world-system theory, Marxist theory provides a cogent analysis of the dynamics of the laws of capitalist development from which it develops its interpretation of the role of imperialism in the context of the global dimensions of the capitalist mode. Hence, the latter approach, based on its concrete understanding of these laws, is rooted in Marxist political economy, while world-system theory, supplementing an eclectic perspective with a selective and inconsistent use of (neo-) Marxist terminology, has led to much confusion (Hoogvelt 1982, 171–207).[4]

I would argue that, since it attempts to explain imperialism and globalization from the perspective of particular regions or nations in a subjectivist political formulation, rather than an objective economic one as viewed from the angle of the laws of motion of transnational capital from its inception in the imperial centers, the world-system approach is essentially incompatible with Marxism. The formulation of the question in these national terms thus leads world-system theory to a conclusion opposite to that of Marxism in that, while Marxist theory provides us a dynamic conception of capitalist development, including its inherent class contradictions that lead to class struggles, world-system theory lends itself to a static conception with respect to the internal laws of the changing capitalist mode (see Larrain 1989, 188–211).

If, as in the world-system approach, the ultimate units of analysis are nations and national institutional structures (and not classes and class struggles), then clearly one is not engaging in class analysis. In instances when classes are discussed by followers of this approach, they are done so in an eclectic, arbitrary fashion, as the following statement by one of its leading spokespersons indicates:

> Turning to the underdeveloped countries, specifically to those of Latin America, I may hazard the following general observations. The proletariat includes most of the participants in the economic system. It most certainly includes the peasants, "subsistence" peasants included. Also the steadily employed workers, casually employed workers be they urban or rural (in case one doesn't want to call the latter "peasants"), most of the members of the "middle classes," urban and rural. (Frank 1975, 94)

Marxist theory, on the other hand, grasps the class nature of imperialist expansion in dialectical terms, that is, the reality of its (selective) industrialization of the Third World through industrial/manufacturing investments and its simultaneous exploitation of the working class on a world scale. Thus, lacking a clear understanding of the nature of class relations—instead, emphasizing the institutional aspects of imperialist domination and "surplus extraction"—the world-system theory ultimately fails to provide a concrete analysis of the social relations of production in the period of the globalization of capital and capitalist relations as manifested in specific Third World social formations (Petras 1982, 148–155). This mislocation of the source of the problematic leads to erroneous and conflicting political conclusions, as we shall see later.

SUBSTANTIVE ISSUES

The central contribution of the Marxist theory of imperialism is its objective analysis of the laws of motion of the capitalist mode of production. It views capitalist development as rooted in its own internal (class) contradictions. This means that as capitalism develops so do its various forms of exploitation (both within and between specific social formations), and the nature of imperialist exploitation varies in accordance with the nature of the specific class structure of Third World social formations with which imperialism comes into contact. Hence, within this framework, it is possible to substantiate the different stages of capitalist development and the mechanisms that are particular to each stage: the period of colonization and primitive accumulation, involving the plunder of economically backward precapitalist areas; the period of the internationalization of the circuit of commodity-capital, involving the blockage of industrialization in the Third World; and the period of the internationalization of the circuit of productive-capital, involving the industrialization of the

Third World and the exploitation of wage-labor (see Warren 1980; Barkin 1982, 156–161).

On the other hand, viewing this process within a static (undialectical) framework, the world-system theory has been unable to account for changes in the advanced capitalist economy of the center states or for its development, especially in its expansion across national boundaries, which is, of course, one of numerous but key manifestations of the very dynamics of capital accumulation itself. Instead, like dependency theory, it has attempted to explain change in terms of the dynamics of underdevelopment in the Third World from the angle of the less developed countries, stressing the external dependence of Third World nations on successive European and North American "metropolises" or "core" states as the main cause of the former's structural underdevelopment. In this view, the development of the Third World thus becomes subject to the imperialist mechanisms of economic and political/military control, and changes occur only or mainly in the successive forms of imperialist control, oppression, and domination (i.e., from colonialism to imperialism to neocolonialism or neoimperialism), while the substance of that control, underdevelopment, and domination (defined in national, regional, or global terms) remains constant (Werker 1985).

The conceptualization of the problem in these geographic, structural, and institutional terms again leads to the mistaken conclusion of the statics of the system. From the perspective of the world-system theory, however, which takes the world system and the underdeveloped countries within it as the main units of analysis, relations of domination are viewed as dynamic, whereas capitalism and the center's monopoly capitalist structure are not (Roxborough 1979, 55–69). This line of reasoning leaves the impression that capitalism, having reached its highest, imperialist stage, has ceased to be in motion, and, because of its monopoly power in both the core and the periphery, has rid itself of all contradictions, except that between the core and the periphery itself. This undialectical and nonclass conceptualization of the problem has led to much confusion and distortion of Marxism (Leys 1977).

It can be argued that since the central concern in Marxist analysis is the exploitation of labor, there would be little basis for argument among Marxists over formal differences between transnational industrialization ("dependent capitalism") and national industrialization (that led by the national, petit, or "state" bourgeoisie[5]), as in fact both are governed by the capitalist law of profit. The distinction, therefore, between transnational capitalist industrialization and national capitalist industrialization (aside from the former's "distorted" nature, versus the "integrated" and "diversified" nature of local capitalism in the absence of imperialist domination) is grossly exaggerated, as both forms of industrialization are subject to the laws of the capitalist mode of production, which facilitate capital accumulation for the transnational and/or the national bourgeoisie and prolong capitalist class rule (Warren 1980). Under either form of industrialization, the appropriation of surplus value by the capitalist class continues and expands as an increasing number of peasants and marginal segments of the population are drawn into wage-labor employment. Thus, the de facto emphasis on the "progressive" nature of national (as opposed to transnational) capital, and the claim that therefore the critique of "blockage" by imperialism of the national industrialization process should, in effect, be the focus of analysis, as has been the case in most studies adopting such a view, is, I believe, misconceived and misdirected; in practice, they may also lead to wrong (nationalist and class-collaborationist) politics.[6]

It is clear that part of the problem in the disagreement between the two sets of theories stems from the differential definition of the concepts "industrialization" and "development." Industrialization, to the world-system theory, means the material outcome of an integrated and diversified national economy based on the model of classical European capitalist development after the period of primitive accumulation. The "lack" of industrialization in the Third World today, according to this theory, is a manifestation of (1) the unavailability to the Third World bourgeoisie of the conditions of development that were available to European capital at the time of its inception and maturation from the eighteenth to the twentieth centuries and (2) the imperialist "blockage" of industrialization in the Third World, which "postpones" or "eliminates" the possibility of an independent, diversified national capitalist development. This formulation leads one to the erroneous conclusion that the problem of underdevelopment would be overcome once the "inhibiting" forces of imperialist control are eliminated—that is, to achieve "independent" or "autonomous" development, all one needs to do is to "break with the world system." This is certainly the implication of the analysis provided by most dependency and world-system theorists, including Andre Gunder Frank, Immanuel Wallerstein, and Samir Amin.[7]

Continuing this line of argument in his book *Delinking: Towards a Polycentric World* (1990), Amin advocates a complete break in links with the imperial center in favor of "autonomous," "independent" development. The crucial determinant of the social content of such "delinking," however, is the class nature of the forces leading society and the nature and direction of a particular formation defined by the dominant mode of production, and not "delinking" per se for some unspecified "autonomous" form of development, devoid of any clear conception of class.

Conceptualizing capitalism as a global system, Frank, Wallerstein, and Amin have thus freed themselves from the obligation of adopting a class analysis approach to study social formations and their dominant mode(s) of production within definite national/societal boundaries. Such reformulation of earlier dependency theory by adherents of the world-system approach, who have reconceptualized global socioeconomic relations at the world systemic level, has further led to the development of more recent positions that have advocated "disengagement" from the world system.[8] In all of these approaches, however, the units of analysis have remained abstract, systemic forces that operate on a global level, rather than concrete classes and class struggles that take place in concrete social formations. Such abstract formulations of the world systemic problematic has, in effect, led to idealist, populist conceptualizations of systemwide rebellions and revolutions that never seem to happen on a systemwide basis. Clearly, given the historically specific experiences of societies at different stages of development, one cannot expect a uniform, systemwide, simultaneous response to the forces dominating the world system. Thus, taken together, these approaches have yielded the same net result in terms of their political implications: the failure to mobilize the social forces affected by this process to challenge and transform the world system.

Contrary to the inability of the world-system approach to deal with this situation, I would argue that the main problem faced by working people the world over is international capitalism, for it exploits wage-labor at global proportions: The class struggle between labor and capital in this period of the globalization of capital has become the principal contradiction of capitalism on a world scale in both the imperial centers and the Third World. And the mobilization of class forces around this principal contradiction opens the way for a concrete challenge to the global capitalist system that is both real and possible.

CONCLUSION

I have argued here that it is not "underdevelopment," "unequal exchange," "blockage," or "exploitative relations between the core and the periphery" that constitute the primary contradiction of global capitalism today (although all of these factors are important in the comprehensive treatment of the political economy of global capitalism at the present conjuncture). Rather, the primary contradiction of the world capitalist system in this period of the globalization of capital is rooted in relations of production and exploitation (i.e., class relations) on a world scale that are manifested in class struggles in specific social formations throughout the world.

This means that the working class (and its allies) faces exploitation and oppression at both ends of the imperialist capitalist system. Opposition to the monopoly capitalist bourgeoisie in the imperial center is thus organically linked to opposition to the same monopoly capitalist (imperialist) bourgeoisie and its local reactionary allies in the Third World. The Third World workers, then, instead of confronting imperialism as an alien force that manipulates national economies from the "outside," in fact confront it on the very soil of their countries and identify it—much as they do "their own" national bourgeoisie—as an exploiting class that extracts surplus value/profits.

The deeper the imperialist penetration of the Third World, the more numerous, the stronger, and the more organized is the Third World working class, which adopts proletarian ideology and political outlook in forming a genuine challenge to global capitalism. The further the process of the globalization of productive capital, the sharper the contradictions between global capital and Third World wage-labor. And the more forceful the class struggle in the Third World, the deeper and more pervasive globally the contradictions of imperialism, which force it to increase its level of exploitation in the center as well, thus leading to increased class struggles and revolutionary conditions throughout the center states. Cornered by a strong and determined working class at both ends, imperialism thus resorts to an all-out reaction and attempts to stifle and block the movement of international labor. By doing so, however, it further accentuates the contradictions between labor and capital at all fronts, thus preparing its own demise on a global level.

These and other related contradictions of global capitalism are examined in detail in the chapters that follow.

NOTES

1. For theoretical and empirical arguments developed around this thesis, see Warren (1973, 3–45; 1980); Szymanski (1974, 20–40; 1981); Clawson (1977). For a more recent reformulation of this position, see Petras and Veltmeyer (2001).

2. For a critique of circulationist arguments advanced by world-system theorists, see Brenner (1977); see also Roxborough (1979, chapter 4) and Smith (1983, 73–86).

3. For example, see the works of Samir Amin and other world-system theorists. For an elaboration on this point, see Amin (1990a, 1990b, 1997).

4. See also Gulalp (1983, 114–136) and Blomstrom and Hettne (1984, chapters 2–4, 8).

5. National bourgeoisie is the segment of the local capitalist class that owns/controls the means of industrial production that is nationally based. Petit bourgeoisie

make up the self-employed small business sector, including professionals, middle-level government bureaucrats, and intermediate sectors of society in general.

6. On this point, see O'Brien (1973).

7. See the various essays in Limqueco and McFarlane (1983) and Chilcote (1982); see also Oxaal, Barnett, and Booth (1975); Munck (1984); Kay (1989).

8. In addition to Amin (1990a), see Mahjoub (1990).

Chapter Four

The Postwar Rise of U.S. Capital onto the Global Scene

There have been two major turning points in the recent economic history of the United States: one marked the rise to world prominence of the U.S. economy at the conclusion of World War II, when the United States came to lead the global economy in the immediate postwar period; the other signaled the end of "the American century" less than three decades later, when the U.S. economy plunged into an irreversible decline in the early 1970s. Thus, the period from 1945 to the 1970s has been characterized as the heyday of the United States' dominant position in the global economy.

In this chapter, I examine the rise of U.S. capital onto the global scene, the role of the U.S. state in promoting the development and expansion of U.S. capital in the postwar period, and the increasing monopoly control in the U.S. and world economy that gave rise to a new set of contradictions in late twentieth- and early twenty-first-century global capitalism.

THE RISE OF U.S. CAPITAL
ONTO THE GLOBAL SCENE

The origins of U.S. capitalist expansion on a world scale go back to the turn of the twentieth century, when U.S. direct investment abroad amounted to nearly a billion dollars, reaching $1.6 billion by 1908; by 1920, it totaled nearly $4 billion (Lewis 1938, 605–606). The post–World War I prosperity, which ushered in the Roaring Twenties, set U.S. capital on its way to a prominent position within the global economy.

Although the Great Depression of the 1930s did dramatically slow down this expansion and greatly affected the rate of growth of the U.S. economy,

57

both domestically and globally, U.S. entry into World War II and the accompanying wartime contracts provided by the U.S. state to the emerging U.S. transnational monopolies in the early 1940s once again propped up the U.S. economy and turned it into a giant productive machine with extensive operations in distant corners of the world. Thus, by 1950, U.S. foreign direct investment reached $12 billion (U.S. Department of Commerce 1981).

With the decline of the British Empire and the weakening of the rival European economies in the aftermath of World War II, the United States clearly emerged as the leading center of the capitalist world and came to establish its dominant position as a global superpower. U.S. domination of the global economy and policy in the postwar period went virtually unchallenged for nearly three decades, as both Europe and Japan, as well as most underdeveloped peripheral regions of the world, came under direct U.S. economic and/or political-military control (Magdoff 1992).

During the period since 1950, U.S. foreign direct investment increased immensely, climbing from $12 billion in 1950, to $124 billion in 1975, to $1.4 trillion in 2000; together with all other types of investment, total U.S. private investments abroad reached $6 trillion in 2000 (U.S. Department of Commerce, July 2001, 14–15). However, much of this increase was the result of reinvestment of earnings from pervious investments, rather than of new capital flows from the United States into the recipient countries. In fact, outflow of capital from the United States has been only a small fraction of the increase in total foreign direct investment assets. While direct investment income of U.S. corporations was twice the value of outflows in the 1950s, by 2000 the gap between inflows and outflows reached such vast proportions that it became clear that direct investment income, totaling about $105 billion in 1999, was generated mainly through the internal processes of capital accumulation by the transnational subsidiaries within the host countries. Moreover, U.S. transnational monopolies through this process established a system of transnational production that no longer required the flow of capital from the parent to the subsidiaries for branch-plant expansion.

U.S. economic expansion abroad during this period was a logical outcome of the process of capitalist development in the United States for nearly a century; it also coincided with changes in the global balance of forces that permitted U.S. capital to enter the world stage (Dowd 1977). Thus, while the decline of British and, more generally, European power at the conclusion of World War II provided new opportunities for U.S. capital in previously colonized peripheral regions of the world, it also opened up vast areas of economic expansion within Europe itself through the Marshall Plan (the rebuilding of Western Europe through extensive U.S. aid).[1]

The Marshall Plan provided an unprecedented impetus for U.S. corporate expansion in Western Europe in the postwar period. It effectively subsidized and promoted the growth and development of U.S. capital in Europe and set the stage for subsequent capitalist expansion throughout the rest of the world (Kidron 1970). Michael Tanzer states that

> [s]ince war-torn Europe and Japan were heavily dependent upon U.S. assistance for reconstruction, the [U.S.] oil companies and the U.S. government used this opportunity to virtually ram American-controlled oil down the throats of the world to replace coal. Thus, Walter Levy, head of the Marshall Plan's oil division, and previously an economist for Mobil, noted in 1949 that "without ECA [the Marshall Plan] American oil business in Europe would already have been shot to pieces," and commented that "ECA does not believe that Europe should save dollars or even foreign exchange by driving American oil from the European market." Some $2 billion of total Marshall Plan assistance of $13 billion was for oil imports, while the Marshall Plan blocked projects for European crude oil production and helped American oil companies to gain control of Europe's refineries. (1974, 17–18)

Similarly, the establishment by U.S. capital of large-scale production, distribution, and communication networks on the continent strengthened the hand of the United States in Western Europe and thereby helped U.S. business dominate the West European economies throughout the postwar period. Thus, U.S. direct investment in Western Europe increased from a mere $1.7 billion in 1950, to $6.6 billion in 1960, to $25 billion in 1970, to $96 billion in 1980, to $204 billion in 1990, to $649 billion in 2000 (U.S. Department of Commerce, July 2001, 27).

This expansion by U.S. capital was accompanied by an infusion of other investment into Canada, Australia, Japan, and the less developed countries of the Third World, which, together with such investment in Western Europe, reached an immense level. Western Europe accounted for nearly one-half of all U.S. direct investments in the world, indicating its central role in the global operations of the U.S. monopolies, especially in the most recent stage of the latter's postwar expansion throughout the world.

To facilitate its economic objectives in Western Europe, U.S. capital utilized the powers of its state to establish a permanent presence there through a military occupation force bolstered by the North Atlantic Treaty Organization (NATO) and other instruments of imperial domination and control.[2] In this way, Europe was effectively turned into a colonial outpost of the rising U.S. imperial state at the service of U.S. capital now operating on a global scale. Thus, during the immediate postwar period in the late 1940s and early 1950s, the United States rapidly established its dominant position in the world political economy and groomed itself as the leading global superpower exerting control and influence throughout much of the capitalist world (Green 1971; Perlo 1988).

THE ROLE OF THE STATE IN PROMOTING
THE EXPANSION OF U.S. CAPITAL

An important aspect of the state's supportive role toward capital in this process of global expansion was the close relationship between capital and the state resulting from the granting to U.S. business lucrative government contracts for war production during World War II. Thus, by 1944 government purchases of goods and services were seven times greater than they had been in 1939. With the onset of the Cold War after the end of World War II, this relationship grew throughout the postwar period. More specifically, in 1958 military purchases accounted for 93.7 percent of the output of the aircraft industry, 60.7 percent of the ships and boats built, 38.5 percent of transportation equipment production, 38 percent of the output of radio and communications equipment industry, 20.9 percent of electrical machinery, 20.1 percent of instruments, 13.3 percent of primary metals production, and 10.4 percent of petroleum output (Nathanson 1969, 211). Focusing on the industrial-commercial electronics industry, we find that

> 40 percent of all computers installed up to 1959 were purchased directly by the military or by the weapons industry with government funds. In terms of dollar sales, military purchases were even more significant than the 40 percent figure indicates, since they mainly involved large computers. And in one sense, the entire computer market can be traced to the military, since military requirements financed and directed most of the research and development.
>
> What is true for computers applies equally to other large segments of the industrial-commercial electronics market, such as test and measurement equipment and industrial control instruments. Together with computers, these items make up 65 percent of the industrial market. . . .
>
> Altogether then, indirect and direct military demand may account for close to 70 percent of the total output of the $14-billion-a-year electronics industry. This is just the reverse of the market situation in 1950, when consumer products possessed over 60 percent of the market and military products about 20 percent. Since then consumer sales have increased only about $500 million while military sales have increased more than $7 billion. (210)

Clearly, it was through such increases in military purchases that a substantial portion of the postwar U.S. economic growth was sustained. Thus, as Paul

A. Baran and Paul M. Sweezy point out, "the difference between the deep stagnation of the 1930s and the relative prosperity of the 1950s is fully accounted for by the vast military outlays of the 50s" as the U.S. state came to play a critical role in the growth and development of capitalism in the United States during this crucial period of the rise to world prominence of U.S. monopoly capital (1966, 176). By the mid-1960s, U.S. big business became thoroughly transformed into what Dwight D. Eisenhower had earlier called "the military-industrial complex": 20 to 30 percent of the annual sales of major electronics firms like RCA, Magnavox, Philco, Sylvania, Motorola, Westinghouse, and General Electric were in the military-space field; others, like Raytheon, Lear, and General Precision Equipment were selling over 80 percent of their output to the military (Nathanson 1969, 212). Of the five hundred largest industrial corporations in the United States in the mid-1960s, "*at least* 205 [were] significantly involved in military production, either through their primary industry of production, through diversification into the defense sector, or through military research and development contracts. If we exclude from the top 500 the large number of food, apparel, and tobacco firms, then military production involves about 50 percent of the major firms in the economy" (231).

The 1950s and 1960s thus became the "golden age" of U.S. capitalism—a period that can be characterized as a bonanza for big business. The super-profits obtained from overseas investments, government contracts, and intensified exploitation of wage-labor at home and abroad resulted in record profits. Except for several short-term downturns in the business cycle, including four major recessions, this period was generally one of growth and expansion, especially for the largest and most viable U.S. corporations. Taking the performance of the five hundred largest industrial corporations as a yardstick for the overall sales and profit structure of U.S. big business from 1954 to 1980, we find that both in current and constant dollars, sales and profits showed a steady increase during this period (*Fortune* 1989, 347). The growth and expansion of U.S. capital during the 1950s and 1960s strengthened the hand of big business and led to the demise of many smaller businesses, thus resulting in the further monopolization of the U.S. economy (Amoroso 2001).

INCREASING MONOPOLY CONTROL
IN THE U.S. ECONOMY

The postwar period witnessed an accelerated monopolization in the already heavily concentrated and centralized U.S. economy. The process of transnational economic expansion was largely the outcome of the growth and expansion of the giant monopolies in the United States, which, through mergers and acquisitions, came to account for a substantial share of the total assets, sales, and profits during this period (Sherman 1987; Perlo 1988; Berberoglu 1992a).

In a report on two decades of economic activity (1954–1974) by the five hundred largest industrial corporations in the United States, an analyst for *Fortune* magazine writes, "The conglomerates . . . were rapidly piecing together vast empires of astonishing diversity and, in the process, taking over scores of well-known companies. . . . The merger boom meant, of course, that some companies were scoring tremendous sales gains. . . . Over the course of the two decades, the total annual sales of the 500 leaped from $136.8 billion to $834 billion—an average annual growth rate of 9.5 percent" (Martin 1975, 239, 241). It is not surprising, therefore, that the assets of the five hundred largest U.S. corporations increased from 55 percent of the U.S. total in 1955, to 75 percent in 1965, to more than 88 percent in 1980; likewise, sales increased from 58 percent of the U.S. total in 1955, to 65 percent in 1970, to 86 percent in 1980; and, finally, profits rose from 45 percent of the U.S. total in 1955, to 54 percent in 1970, to 88 percent in 1980 (U.S. Council of Economic Advisers and *Fortune,* various years).[3]

The latest available data for 2001 for the five hundred largest U.S. corporations indicate that the assets of the top five hundred increased to $19.1 trillion, revenues to $7.4 trillion, and profits to $264 billion, accounting for 46 percent of total assets and 35.3 percent of total profits in the United States (*Fortune* 2002; U.S. Council of Economic Advisers 2002).[4] Breaking down the data further, the top twenty-five corporations accounted for 31.3 percent of the assets, 29.8 percent of the revenues, and 35.3 percent of the profits of the top five hundred corporations; the top fifty corporations accounted for 44.6 percent of the assets, 42.6 percent of the revenues, and 53.9 percent of the profits of the top five hundred corporations; and the top one hundred corporations accounted for 64.5 percent of the assets, 59.6 percent of the revenues, and 67.6 percent of the profits of the top five hundred corporations in 2001 (*Fortune* 2002). These figures reveal an enormous level of concentration and centralization of capital in the hands of the largest corporations in the United States today.

The process of postwar U.S. monopolization of the economy was not restricted to the industrial, financial, and service sectors alone; agriculture, too, experienced a similar process of consolidation, as fewer and fewer farming units (increasingly formed into giant agricultural conglomerates) came to control a larger and larger acreage, hence a disproportionate share of total assets and cash receipts from farming. In the period 1940 to 1997, the number of farms declined from 6.5 million in 1940 to 1.9 million in 1997, while the average size of farms rose from 170 acres in 1940 to 487 acres in 1997 (U.S. Bureau of the Census 2000, 666). Thus, the largest industrial and agricultural corporations have now reached a stage wherein they can rightly be characterized as monopoly and operating through the logic of monopoly.

NEW CONTRADICTIONS

While the *effects* of accelerated monopolization in the United States and U.S. transnational expansion abroad began to appear in the U.S. domestic economy as early as the 1970s and became fully visible by the early 1980s, competition from other rival centers of world capitalism began to pose a challenge to U.S. global economic dominance during this period, as a number of rising capitalist states emerged as serious contenders on the world scene (Beams 1998; O'Meara, Mehlinger, and Krain 2000; Halliday 2001). Japan and West Germany, and the European Union as a whole, as well as a number of newly industrializing countries (e.g., South Korea, Taiwan, Hong Kong, and Singapore) began to make headway in production and worldwide trade and together surpassed the traditional U.S. position as the preeminent global economic power in the postwar world economy (Weber 2001; Hook and Harukiyo 2001). Thus, beginning in the early 1970s and throughout the subsequent period, U.S. monopoly capital began to experience an entirely different process of global economic relations—one that was to set into motion a new set of contradictions that favored its global economic rivals (Sklair 2002).

Throughout the 1980s and 1990s, the world political economy went through a series of complex transformations from one region to another: accelerated U.S. global expansion during this period was accompanied by economic decline and class polarization in the domestic front; the collapse of the former Soviet Union and its associated East European states was in stark contrast to the economic boom in China through joint ventures and mass production for the world market; and the integration of European states into the European Union was in sharp contrast to the turmoil in the Balkans, the Middle East, and elsewhere in the Third World where we have seen a rise in nationalism and ethnic conflict that has torn apart the social fabric of entire societies (Halliday 2001).

The culmination of these and other developments around the world during the final decades of the twentieth century have brought to the fore a new set of contradictions arising from the logic of transnational capitalist expansion. It is to the analysis of these new contradictions to which I turn in the next chapter.

NOTES

1. The Marshall Plan, proposed by then secretary of state General George Marshall in June 1947, was implemented the following year as the European Recovery Program. In its four years of operation, the program gave $13 billion to eighteen West European nations (including Greece and Turkey) for a broad variety of investment projects. Over 70 percent of the amount was spent for American goods (Dowd 1977, 235).

2. NATO was established in 1949 as the military counterpart of the Marshall Plan.

3. The relationship between monopolization based on asset size and the domination of markets and a tendency for profits to rise has been shown widely in a number of studies. One such study, conducted at Harvard University in the 1970s, which covered 57 corporations involved in 620 separate businesses, found that the greater the share of the market for a given product that a company monopolized, the higher its rate of profit. Thus, according to the findings of this study, companies controlling less than 7 percent of the market share reported a 9.6 percent return on investment, while those controlling 22 to 36 percent of the market reported a 17.9 percent return, and companies controlling over 36 percent of the market showed a 30.2 percent profit (Cappo 1977, 28).

4. The amount for total profits of the top five hundred corporations excludes J. D. S. Uniphase (no. 477 on the *Fortune 500* list), which lost $56.1 billion in profits in 2001 (*Fortune* 2002, F-19).

Chapter Five

The Globalization of U.S.
Capital and the Resurgence
of Interimperialist Rivalry

It is one of the great ironies of our time that imperialism, that is, monopoly capitalism operating on a world scale, would promote the spread of capitalism throughout the world, while at the same time giving rise to a new set of contradictions at the global and national levels. In this chapter, I take up an analysis of the globalization of U.S. capital and the resurgence of interimperialist rivalry, while in a subsequent chapter I examine the contradictions of this process as it affects the U.S. economy at the national level.

One major result of the international expansion of U.S. capital during the postwar period, which was intensified and reached unprecedented proportions by the mid-1970s, has been the emergence of new centers of world capitalism (Western Europe and Japan) and the resurgence of global, interimperialist rivalry. Such rivalry between the leading capitalist states has its roots in U.S. postwar domination of the economies of Western Europe and Japan during the second half of the twentieth century.[1]

THE POSTWAR GLOBALIZATION OF U.S. CAPITAL
AND CONTROL OF THE WORLD ECONOMY

Although the large-scale U.S. postwar global expansion ushered in a period of unquestioned U.S. supremacy over the world economy and polity during the 1950s and 1960s, the economic strength of U.S. capital over foreign markets through investment, production, and trade during the 1970s took on a new significance—one resulting from the restructuring of the international division of labor. U.S. transnational capital, in line with its transfer of large segments of the production process to the periphery, poured massive amounts of capital into select areas of the Third World, as well as into its traditional bases of foreign investment—Canada and Western Europe—and became the leading center of world capitalism in a new way, that is, by becoming the dominant force in the worldwide production process. Thus, not only did overall U.S. direct investment expand immensely during this period, but also a shift in the form of investment in favor of manufacturing came to constitute the new basis of changes in the international division of labor (Berberoglu 1987b).

Whereas total U.S. foreign direct investment from 1960 to 1970 more than doubled, from $32.7 billion in 1960 to $75.5 billion in 1970, it nearly tripled during the 1970s, reaching $213.5 billion in 1980; by 2000, it reached $1.4 trillion (U.S. Department of Commerce, July 2001, 27). And while petroleum and manufacturing investments accounted for the same proportion of the total, at $11 billion each in 1960, and petroleum investments roughly doubled twice during the following two decades, reaching $19.8 billion in 1970, $47 billion in 1980, and then $105 billion in 2000, manufacturing investments nearly tripled twice during this same period, reaching $31 billion in 1970, $89 billion in 1980, and finally $344 billion in 2000 (U.S. Bureau of the Census, various issues; U.S. Department of Commerce, July 2001, 27).

More significantly, while total aggregate investment dollars in these sectors continued to flow into the developed capitalist countries (primarily Canada and Western Europe), the manufacturing sector of both developed and less developed countries received a disproportionate share of total investments, far surpassing those in the petroleum industry throughout this period. Thus, investments in manufacturing increased from $9.2 billion in 1960, to $25.6 billion in 1970, to $71.4 billion in 1980, to $254 billion in 2000 in the developed capitalist countries, and from $1.9 billion in 1960, to $5.5 billion in 1970, to $17.7 billion in 1980, to $89.7 billion in 2000 in the less developed countries (U.S. Department of Commerce, September 2001, 90). Moreover, these investments were concentrated in few key countries within each region. In the developed capitalist world, Canada, Britain, Germany, the Netherlands, and France accounted for the bulk of these investments; in the less developed capitalist periphery, Brazil, Mexico, and Singapore accounted for the bulk of these investments.

Historically, in the earlier stages of capitalist development, imperial investments have generally tended to be concentrated in the raw materials sector. And this was true for the United States up until the early 1960s. During the period since 1960, a shift in emphasis from raw materials to manufacturing investments has taken place, and the manufacturing sector has clearly emerged as *the* major category of U.S. direct investment abroad (Petras and Veltmeyer 2001).

Focusing on the less developed countries, we see that in 1960 U.S. foreign raw materials investments amounted to $7 billion, while manufacturing investments totaled less than $2 billion. However, from the early 1960s on, the relative share of the raw materials sector began to decline significantly, as manufacturing investments began to rise very rapidly. This trend began to take effect during the 1960s and especially since the early 1970s, when the relative share of raw materials investments declined from 60.7 percent of the total in 1960 to 12.1 percent in 2000, while the share of manufacturing investments rose from 17 percent of the total in 1960 to 27.6 percent in 2000. This was accompanied by a major increase in the amount of financial investments, which rose from $1.5 billion in 1970 to $166.7 billion in 2000, reaching 35.7 percent of all U.S. direct investments in the Third World in 2000 (U.S. Department of Commerce 1981; August 1991, 88; September 2001, 90).[2]

These data clearly show a shift in U.S. direct investments in the Third World from raw materials to manufacturing (and financial) investments. As has been the case in the developed capitalist countries for a long time, a number of less developed countries have reached a stage of economic development where manufacturing investments now represent the single largest category of U.S. foreign direct investment.[3]

In line with this process of expansion in manufacturing investments in Western Europe, Canada, and some regions of the less developed periphery, U.S. transnational capital has made inroads in acquiring an increasing number of local corporations in these regions in an attempt to reduce or eliminate any resistance to its monopoly of the production, distribution, and accumulation process. Thus, we have seen a growing number of U.S. corporate takeovers of prominent European, Japanese, Canadian, Brazilian, and other firms in steel, auto, aerospace, electronics, communications, banking, and other sectors of the world economy over the past three decades (Beams 1998; Halliday 2001).

With the infusion of large sums of investment into Western Europe beginning in the 1960s, U.S.-based transnationals obtained a dominant position in the European computer and electronics industries by the end of the decade, producing 80 percent of the computers, 95 percent of the integrated circuits, and 50 percent of the semiconductors (Servan-Schreiber 1968, 13–14). Throughout the 1970s, the centralization of capital in Western Europe, Canada, and Japan (under U.S. majority ownership and control) intensified, as U.S. firms in other sectors of the economy expanded their operations in a bid to monopolize them as well. Thus by the late 1970s, U.S. foreign direct investment in West Germany reached a predominant position in oil refining (80 percent), glass and cement (54 percent), foods (54 percent), and electrical machinery (51 percent). It also obtained a strong position in iron and metals (50 percent), plastic and rubber (48 percent), pulp, paper, and boards (40 percent), automobiles (37 percent), and chemicals (33 percent), as well as in a number of other sectors at various rates (Szymanski 1981, 501–502). The United States maintained a prominent position in these investments as the leading country in control of the largest share of the total. As of the late 1970s, among West Germany's thirty largest corporations were nine foreign subsidiaries, of which six (Exxon, General Motors [GM], Ford, IBM, Texaco, and Mobil Oil) were U.S. owned. Between 1961 and 1978, about 38 percent of all new foreign direct investment in West Germany was from the United States. In Britain, U.S. transnationals obtained an even better position than in West Germany. In 1977, about 110 of Britain's 500 largest nonfinancial corporations were foreign owned, and two-thirds of the total capital invested in Britain by these corporations was controlled by U.S. and Canadian firms (McBride and Wiseman 2000; Weber 2001).

In Japan in 1970, of the $7 billion in total foreign assets, the U.S. share was between 60 and 70 percent. U.S. firms accounted for 477 of the 776 foreign companies operating in Japan (Halliday and McCormic 1973, 5). In the early 1970s, IBM controlled about 70 percent of Japan's computer market, through a wholly owned subsidiary, National Cash Register Company (Japan). In the petroleum industry, foreign capital, predominantly U.S. capital, controlled over half the Japanese market, while the company with the biggest sales of petroleum products in Japan, Nippon Oil Company, was in partnership with the U.S. giant Caltex. By the end of 1971, U.S. capital had control over the supply of 80 percent of Japanese imports of crude oil. And in agriculture, United Fruit Company moved in late 1971 to raise its holding in the Far East Fruit Company (a joint venture) from 44 percent to 78 percent (Halliday and McCormack 1973, 7). Finally, responding to the expansion of the Japanese car industry into the U.S. market, U.S. car manufacturers, such as GM and Chrysler, moved to buy into the Japanese motor vehicle industry, where GM tied up with Isuzu and Chrysler with Mitsubishi, both capturing over one-third of the stock of these companies, while Ford captured 25 percent of the stock of Mazda. Thus, throughout the 1970s an increasing number of U.S. companies expanded into various branches of Japanese industry (e.g., steel, electronics, high technology) in an effort to control competitors at the source, while at the same time effecting protectionist measures through high tariffs to seal the U.S. market against the influx of massive imports from rival firms (O'Meara, Mehlinger, and Krain 2000).[4]

In Canada, by the mid-1970s foreign capital controlled 54 percent of the manufacturing sector, including 69 percent of the electrical products industry, 73 percent of the chemical industry, 92 percent of the petroleum and coal industry, 67 percent of nonelectrical machinery, and 40 percent of paper and related products. And U.S.-controlled companies accounted for about 75 percent of the total assets of all foreign-controlled corporations (Szymanski 1981, 502; Berberoglu 1992b).

In Brazil in the late 1970s, foreign firms (mostly U.S. firms) accounted for the production of 60 percent of heavy machinery, 80 percent of radio and television sets, 90 percent of pharmaceuticals, 95 percent of autos, and 100 percent of tire and rubber products (Berberoglu 1987b, 69). The situation is similar in a number of other Third World countries (Maitra 1996).

The penetration of U.S. capital into Western Europe, Canada, Japan, and selected Third World countries in the 1970s resulted in the further centralization of local capital in the hands of U.S. transnationals, effecting greater control over these crucial markets as well as protecting the U.S. market from its competitors, while turning the West European, Japanese, Canadian, and Third World economies into appendages of a world economy dominated by the U.S. monopolies. In this way, the U.S. transnationals succeeded, by the late 1970s, in dominating the world's production, trade, and financial networks.

Reacting to this situation during the 1980s, Western Europe and Japan have made a comeback to counter the domination of their economies by U.S. capital and thus entered center stage in a new round of global interimperialist rivalry for control of the financial lifeline of the world capitalist economy (Beams 1998).

THE RESURGENCE OF INTERIMPERIALIST RIVALRY

The arena of this new rivalry between the major capitalist powers, which began to unfold in full force during the 1980s, extends from Western Europe, to North America, to Japan, to select regions of the Third World, while new areas outside these regions, such as China, Eastern Europe, and the former Soviet Union, may become forces that tip the balance in favor of one or another of the capitalist rivals fighting it out on the global scene (see Berberoglu 1992a).

The decline of the U.S. economy, beginning in the mid-1970s, coincided with the rise of Europe organized into a viable economic force during this period. The expansion of the European Economic Community (EEC) via the Common Market on the continent during the 1970s set the stage for the emergence of Western Europe as a serious contender for the leadership of the world capitalist economy. Thus, while U.S. capital was in the process of becoming increasingly internationalized and spreading across a vast global territory constituting the new boundaries of a new international division of labor dependent on the U.S. monopolies, Europe focused on its home base in expanding the basis of a giant market of some four hundred million relatively well-off consumers that would constitute the basis of a mass industrial expansion process that may during the first decade of the twenty-first century shift the center of economic power from North America to the European heartland.[5]

A similar development in East Asia and the Pacific Rim brought about the rise to economic prominence of Japan and a number of newly industrializing countries such as South Korea, Taiwan, Hong Kong, and Singapore. Japan's successful entry into the global economic scene during the past two decades has bore fruit in a big way, as Japanese banks captured, by 1988, a position where nine of the top ten banks in the world were Japanese—quite a contrast with the position of Japan in the world economy in the mid-1970s.

In 1974, the three largest banks in the world were American (BankAmerica Corporation, Citicorp, and Chase Manhattan) while only two of the top ten banks were Japanese (Dai-Ichi Kangyo, ranked fifth, and Sumitomo, ranked tenth). However, a little over a decade later, in 1988, nine out of the ten largest banks in the world were Japanese, while only one U.S. bank (Citicorp) remained in the top twenty-five list. In all, of the twenty-five largest banks in the world in 1988, seventeen were Japanese, seven were European (four French, two British, and one West German), and one American. By 1991, all of the top ten banks in the world were Japanese, while only one U.S. bank remained in the top twenty-five list. Clearly, by the end of the 1980s and early 1990s Japanese banks came to dominate international finance capital and established themselves as the leading force in the world of finance.

A similar trend in the position of industrial corporations over the past two decades has resulted in a decline in number of U.S. corporations and an increase in number of Japanese and European corporations in the top twenty-five list. Thus, while in 1974 fifteen of the twenty-five largest industrial corporations in the world were U.S.-based, by 1988 this number was down to nine; conversely, while in 1974 there were only eight European corporations and only one Japanese corporation among the twenty-five largest industrial corporations in the world, by 1988 these numbers increased to eleven and four, respectively. Moreover, if we take European and Japanese corporations together as posing a challenge to U.S. dominance of the world economy, we see a complete reversal of the situation in 1988 as compared with 1974. Whereas the share of U.S. corporations in the top twenty-five list declined from fifteen in 1974 to nine in 1988, the share of European and Japanese corporations increased from nine in 1974 to fifteen in 1988. This trend continued to unfold during the 1990s, placing the European and Japanese corporations in an increasingly favorable position vis-à-vis their U.S. counterparts.

These developments clearly show that a shift in centers of the world economy has taken place—away from the United States and toward Japan and Europe, and increasingly China, with Japan controlling the financial lifeline of the global capitalist system and Europe (especially Germany) and Japan making inroads into industrial production, while China captures a growing share of world trade.

With the increase in the number of European and Japanese companies among the top one hundred, and with production moving in the direction of advanced electronics, where Japan has clearly achieved an edge over its U.S. and European competitors, it is not difficult to see that Japanese capital may come to play a central role in the world economy and establish itself as a viable competitor in the decade ahead. This, in conjunction with developments in Western Europe and the potential economic unity of Eastern and Western Europe during the first decade of the twenty-first century, may bring about a multipolar world economy in which the United States constitutes a junior partner stripped of its postwar dominance.

The unprecedented economic and political changes unfolding at full speed during the 1990s have ushered in a new international order in which superpower military tensions have given way to global economic competition and rivalry among the leading capitalist economies, which have arisen during this period over the control of oil in the greater Middle East and the Central Asian region.

INTERIMPERIALIST RIVALRY FOR CONTROL OF OIL IN THE MIDDLE EAST

Over the course of the past two decades, the major imperialist powers of the late twentieth and early twenty-first centuries (the United States, Germany, and Japan) have attempted to use as their surrogate one or another of the major regional powers in the Middle East (Iran, Iraq, and Saudi Arabia) to advance their political and economic interests in the region—above all, in securing access to sources of oil to fuel the industrial engines of their economies and thus maintaining global hegemony over their economic rivals.

In this interimperialist competition between the major capitalist powers, the two rising capitalist states (Germany and Japan) have been attempting to establish independent access to sources of Middle Eastern oil, bypassing the United States' postwar grip over the region through its control of a string of satellite nations from Iran to Saudi Arabia and the Persian Gulf states. The German and Japanese challenge to U.S. domination of Middle Eastern oil prompted a swift response by the United States through massive U.S. military intervention in Saudi Arabia and the invasion of Iraq with the subsequent launching of the Persian Gulf War of 1991—a war that was ostensibly launched to drive the Iraqi army out of Kuwait, but in fact was designed to punish Iraq for its role in cultivating close economic and geopolitical ties with the United States' chief global economic rivals over access to and control of oil in the Middle East (Bresheeth and Yuval-Davis 1991).[6]

The recent U.S. intervention in Afghanistan in the aftermath of the September 11, 2001, attacks on the World Trade Center in New York City and the overthrow of the Taliban regime for harboring the al Qaeda terrorists, as well as the subsequent war against Iraq, and threats against other regimes in what the Bush administration has called the "Axis of Evil," stretching from the Middle East through Southwest Asia to North Korea, is another expression of U.S. power imposed over the region to secure access to sources of oil in the Middle East and *beyond* (Burbach and Clarke 2002). Thus, while the flow of oil from the Middle East continues to play a prominent role in ensuring the United States's dominant position in the region and thereby the world economy, the collapse of the Soviet Union and the emergence of the post-Soviet new independent states, such as Azerbaijan and Turkmenistan, have provided access to alternative sources of oil for the U.S. transnational oil companies, such that a new oil pipeline from the Caspian Sea through Turkmenistan, Afghanistan, and Pakistan to the Indian Ocean would provide an alternative to the oil from the volitile Middle East (Rall 2002, 49). Still, the Middle East remains the centerpiece of U.S. transnational prominence in the global economy, and Iran and Iraq continue to play an important role as the leading regional powers that have been entangled in interimperialist rivalries for control of oil in the Middle East throughout the twentieth and early twenty-first centuries.

Iran, Iraq, and Interimperialist Rivalry in the Middle East

In the period from the early 1950s to the late 1970s—a period of uncontested U.S. supremacy in the Middle East—the United States firmly established itself in Iran and other countries of the Persian Gulf to control the flow of oil from the Middle East (Halliday 1979). By the 1970s, the United States became the chief importer of Iranian oil. Iranian exports to the United States, consisting primarily of crude oil, rose dramatically from $60 million in 1970, to $2.1 billion in 1974, to $4.3 billion in 1978, the final year of the Shah's regime; in turn, imports from the United States rose sharply from $359 million in 1970, to $974 million in 1974, to $4.1 billion in 1978 (International Monetary Fund 1977, 148–149; 1982, 207–208; 1987, 229–230; 1991, 226–227). However, in the latter half of the 1970s interimperialist rivalries between the major capitalist powers began to reappear, as Japan, Germany, Britain, and other major powers began to expand their trade relations with Iran.

Although the U.S. grip over Iran in the postwar period strengthened the Shah's authoritarian rule and kept him in power for twenty-five years, it also prompted his regime to open up to other capitalist powers and to establish Iran as a regional subimperialist power in the Middle East (Halliday 1979; Clawson 1977). Thus, in the latter half of the 1970s Iranian exports (mainly oil) to Japan, Germany, and other European countries dramatically increased, while imports of consumer goods from these countries similarly increased (Sugihara 1993, 1–13).

To counter these developments, Iraq—Iran's chief rival in the region—attracted a number of European countries, such as France and Italy, as well as Japan, to meet their energy needs in exchange for imported manufactured goods—a relationship Iraq sought to cultivate in building itself as an alternative regional power center in the Middle East. As a result, Iraqi exports to Japan, consisting primarily of oil, rose from $5 million in 1972, to $527 million in 1976, to $4 billion in 1980; to France, it increased from $268 million in 1972, to $1.5 billion in 1976, to $5.1 billion in 1980; and to Italy, it rose from $250 million in 1972, to $1.2 billion in 1976, to $2.6 billion in 1980 (International Monetary Fund 1977, 150–151; 1982, 210–211; 1987, 231–232; 1991, 228–229).

The overthrow of the Shah's regime in 1979 and the accession to power of a new Islamic regime in Iran, followed by the war with Iraq, brought import-export trade between Iran and the United States to a virtual halt; but, despite these developments, Iran's trade with Japan, as well as with Germany and other European countries, continued to be on a strong footing throughout the 1980s. Thus, while Iran's exports to the United States dropped from $4.3 billion in 1978, to $556 million in 1982, to a mere $2 million in 1990, exports to Japan made up the bulk of Iran's total exports, amounting to $3.9 billion in 1978, $2.3 billion in 1982, and $3.2 billion in 1990 (International Monetary Fund, 1970–1976, 148–149; 1982, 207–208; 1987, 229–230; 1991, 226–227).

Likewise, while imports from the United States declined from $4.1 billion in 1978, to $209 million in 1983, to $140 million in 1990, imports from Japan totaled $3 billion in 1978, $3.1 billion in 1983, and $1.8 billion in 1990; imports from Germany were also an important part of total Iranian imports, totaling $3.7 billion in 1978, $3.3 billion in 1983, and $2.8 billion in 1990 (International Monetary Fund 1970–1976 148–149; 1982, 207–208; 1987, 229–230; 1991, 226–227).

Clearly, over the past three decades there has occurred a major shift in the export of Iranian oil away from the United States and toward Japan and various European countries. This has been also evident in the source of Iranian imports, such that while there has been a sharp drop in imports from the United States, imports from Japan, Germany, and other European countries have substantially increased over the same period—indicating an apparent shift in patterns of political alliances manifested in import-export trade.

In Iraq, during the early 1980s, we see a similar pattern of trade relations with rival advanced capitalist countries, where Japan, France, and Italy have been the prime recipients of Iraqi oil exports and, together with Germany, the major sources of Iraqi imports of manufactured goods. However, by the late 1980s the United States began to tilt away from Iran and toward Iraq and became the chief purchaser of Iraqi oil and the largest supplier of finished manufactured goods. Iraqi exports to the United States increased from $478 million in 1987, to $1.5 billion in 1988, to $2.3 billion in 1989, to $3 billion in 1990; imports of goods from the United States likewise rose from $752 million in 1987 to $1.3 billion in 1989, dropping to $704 million in 1990 (International Monetary Fund 1970–1976, 150–151; 1982, 210–211; 1987, 231–232; 1991, 228–229).

The rivalry between the chief imperialist powers vis-à-vis access to and business with Iran and Iraq during the 1980s thus became intensified by the decade's end and led to an opening for greater regional power play between the two competing local centers vying for control over the Persian Gulf, hence an increase in their bargaining position vis-à-vis the rival imperialist powers. Iraq's invasion of Kuwait in August 1990, Bernard Headley points out, "had the potential to upset the balance of economic power in the Middle East and threatened the ability of Western (especially U.S. and British) powers to have a decisive influence over the terms and conditions of oil policy" (1991, 322). Thus, to counter such a possible development, Headley writes, the United States wanted to "use its military might to reassert Western control over the world's key resources and to reinforce U.S. strength in relation to its economic rivals" (323). Hence, "Iraq's invasion of Kuwait provided an opportunity to implement this militaristic strategy for making sure the U.S. would be the world's undisputed superpower" (323).

The Persian Gulf War of 1991

The United States went to war against Iraq in order to "liberate" Kuwait, to uphold freedom and the rule of law, and to take a stand against international aggression—so argued the U.S. administration, its Western allies, and its Arab collaborator regimes, which have brutally ruled the region for decades. In his State of the Union address, President George H. W. Bush proclaimed, "What is at stake is . . . a new world order—where diverse nations are drawn together in common cause to achieve the universal aspirations of mankind: peace and security, freedom and the rule of law. . . . Saddam Hussein's unprovoked invasion . . . will not stand" (quoted in Brenner 1991, 122).

If this could happen to the al-Sabah family in Kuwait, the argument went, it could also happen to the Saudi royal family, as well as the sultans and the emirs and their kind throughout the Persian Gulf. This would mean that Saddam Hussein would next march down the Arabian Peninsula and eventually take over Saudi Arabia, then the entire Persian Gulf region, and finally the whole Middle East. But as Edward Greer points out:

> The ground advanced to the American people to accede to attacking Iraq was that of the classical big lie: that the war to be waged was a collective and preemptive defense against a powerful regional criminal state, one with advanced means of mass destruction which it was in the process of deploying against world peace.
>
> In retrospect, the ascribed reasons were false, and known to be such by the president. Iraq was not targeted because Hussein had launched an unprovoked military attack on a neighboring state which has major oil deposits. Saddam Hussein had already done precisely that to Iran a few years before, with active U.S. support.
>
> Nor was Iraq targeted because it was defying United Nations resolutions condemning military aggression and occupation of another sovereign state or its territory. Neither the Turkish occupation of Cyprus, nor the Israeli occupation of the West Bank—both continuing to this day in contravention of similar resolutions—constituted a casus belli for the United States.
>
> Nor was Iraq targeted for American military attack because Kuwait's medieval regime . . . embodied any political or cultural value dear to Americans. (1991, 6–7)

The massive intervention by the United States in the Persian Gulf and the invasion of Iraq, despite proclamations to the contrary, was not for democracy and freedom, "the rule of law," "liberating" Kuwait, peace, security, or a "new" world order. Interestingly enough, it was not for the continued supply of oil to the United States either, for the United States neither depends on nor needs any significant amount of oil from the Middle East, as less than 10 percent of total U.S. oil consumption originates there. Other, more reliable and more secure sources, such as Mexico, Venezuela, and the North Sea, for example, can easily take up the slack. So, why then is the oil question raised at all?

What seems to be a complicated issue becomes clear and revealing once we discover that the oil controlled by the U.S. transnational oil companies in the Middle East is supplied mainly *not* to the United States, but to Germany and Japan—to fuel and thereby control the industrial life of the United States' chief rivals in the world economy. "Germany and Japan are rising economic powers, while Britain and the United States are declining. . . . As rising powers, Germany and Japan were not particularly threatened by Iraq's seizure of Kuwaiti resources. . . . Britain and the United States have had exactly the opposite reaction" (Mayer 1991, 3–4).

As client states of the United States in the Persian Gulf, Kuwait, Saudi Arabia, and the oil emirates play a key role in securing U.S. hegemony in the Middle East, hence controlling the flow of oil from this region. "The abolition of American suzerainty over oil-producing states of the Persian Gulf," writes Tom Mayer, "would threaten . . . the position of the United States relative to its principal commercial rivals" (1991, 4). Thus, "it is hardly surprising that the United States should resort to war to repel a challenge to the imperial status quo. In the traditional fashion of declining economic powers (e.g., fourth-century imperial Rome, late fifteenth-century Spain, pre-First World War Britain), U.S. leaders are continually tempted to compensate for economic weakness with military force" (4).

The significance of control of sources of oil in the Middle East by the United States becomes evident as soon as one considers the alternative: How different the world might actually be if the oil fields now controlled by the U.S. oil companies were in fact controlled by that of Japan and Germany!

The United States and its coalition partners succeeded in punishing Iraq for its invasion of Kuwait by forcing Iraq out of Kuwait and establishing a more firm control over sources of oil in the Middle East. At the same time the regime of Saddam Hussein was kept intact, but a clear message was sent to him and his newly found European and Asian allies to halt their challenge of U.S. power in the Middle East in the post-Soviet "new world order." The challenge to U.S. global supremacy was yet to occur. It came a decade later with the shock of the September 11, 2001, attacks against the symbol of U.S. global economic domination, the twin towers of the World Trade Center in

New York City, and the command and control center of U.S. global military domination, the Pentagon in Washington, D.C. These events of major world-wide significance prompted the massive U.S. military responses, the invasions of Afghanistan in 2001 and Iraq in 2003, actions that were in the making well before the September 11 attacks, but the latter served as the pretext to reassert U.S. global supremacy in the coming period.

The Afghan War of 2001

U.S. military invasion of Afghanistan in late 2001 came in the aftermath of the September 11 attacks on the twin towers of the World Trade Center in New York City and the Pentagon in Washington, D.C. The invasion was carried out in retaliation to the perpetrators of the September 11 attacks, which, according to the U.S. government, were committed by a terrorist group known as al Qaeda based in Afghanistan.

Accusing the Taliban regime in Afghanistan of harboring the al Qaeda terrorists led by Osama bin Laden, the U.S. military launched the invasion, overthrew the Taliban, and carried out a massive bombing campaign that leveled large parts of the country suspected to be al Qaeda hideouts. Thousands of bombs that were dropped on this poor country have caused much devastation, destruction, and death. While several hundred al Qaeda members were killed through this operation, several thousand civilians also perished in pursuit of the group's revered leader, Osama bin Laden, whom the United States has still failed to capture as of this writing in early 2003.[7] But the war in Afghanistan and the United States' presence and engagement in the region did not start with the terrorist attacks on September 11. In fact, it goes back to a much earlier period when the United States was actively involved in shaping events in Afghanistan for over two decades, leading to the accession to power of the Taliban in the mid-1990s (Bonosky 2001; Marsden 2002).

The origins of U.S. intervention in Afghanistan go back to the late 1970s, when in 1978 the corrupt and dictatorial government of President Mohammed Daoud was forced out of office. According to Parenti,

> The new government began to pursue much needed reforms. It legalized labor unions, and set up a minimum wage, a progressive income tax, a literacy campaign, and programs that gave ordinary people greater access to health care, housing and public sanitation. (57)

However, serious opposition arose against the government from several quarters—especially the feudal landlords and the Islamic clergy—and pressure was put on the government to halt the popular reforms and reverse its egalitarian policies:

> The feudal landlords opposed the land reform program that infringed on their holdings while benefitting poor tenant farmers. And tribesmen and fundamentalist mullahs vehemently opposed the government's dedication to gender equality and the education of women and children.
>
> Because of its egalitarian economic policies the government also incurred the opposition of the U.S. national security state. (Parenti 2002b, 57–58)

These were the precipitating events that put Afghanistan on the global map. "Almost immediately after the PDP [the People's Democratic Party] coalition came to power," writes Parenti, "the CIA, assisted by Saudi and Pakistani military, launched a large scale intervention into Afghanistan on the side of the ousted feudal lords, reactionary tribal chieftains, mullahs, and opium traffickers" (2002b, 58).

> Over the years the United States and Saudi Arabia expended about $40 billion on the war in Afghanistan. The CIA and its allies recruited, supplied, and trained almost 100,000 radical mujahideen from forty Muslim countries including Pakistan, Saudi Arabia, Iran, Algeria, and Afghanistan itself. Among those who answered the call was Saudi-born millionaire rightwinger Osama bin Laden and his cohorts. (Parenti 2002b, 58–59, 60)

The constant pressure on the PDP and superior arms provided to the mujahideen by the CIA eventually succeeded in overthrowing the popular government of Afghanistan in 1992, installing in its place a brutal, right-wing Islamic dictatorship of the mujahideen who unleashed an official reign of terror on the people of Afghanistan that was the beginning of a dark period in Afghan history (Bonosky 2001; Marsden 2002).

> Upon taking over Afghanistan, the mujahideen . . . ravaged the cities, terrorized civilian populations, looted, staged mass executions, closed schools, raped thousands of women and girls, and reduced half of Kabul to rubble. . . . Ruling the country gangster-style and looking for lucrative sources of income, the tribes ordered farmers to plant opium poppy. The Pakistani ISI, a close junior partner of the CIA, set up hundreds of heroin laboratories across Afghanistan. (Parenti 2002b, 61)

Soon the Afghan-Pakistan border had become the biggest heroin-producing region in the world. Given its callous behavior and excesses in abuses of the Afghan people, the mujahideen government became very unstable and a liability to the U.S. and Pakistani states to maintain order under its control. Thus, in 1994 U.S. and Pakistani leaders devised a plan to support a group that might bring together the various reactionary elements in the country to form a stable right-wing government; that group was the Taliban (Gohari 2001; Rashid 2002; Marsden 2002). "Within a year," writes Parenti, "an extremist strain of Sunni Islam called the Taliban—heavily funded and advised by the ISI and the CIA and with the support of Islamic political parties in Pakistan—fought its way to power, taking over most of the country, luring many tribal chiefs into its fold with threats and bribes" (2002b, 63).

Once the Taliban came to power, the country changed drastically, *for the worse.* "The Taliban unleashed a religious reign of terror, imposing an even stricter interpretation of Muslim Law than used by most of the Kabul clergy" (Parenti 2002b, 63). But, for the United States the Taliban was a useful tool in its strategy to control the entire Central Asian region.[8]

While it has been revealed by the mainstream mass media that the United States had planned to invade Afghanistan to destroy al Qaeda nine months prior to the attacks on the World Trade Center and the Pentagon,[9] the September 11 events provided the rationale to declare an all-out war against al Qaeda and the Taliban and move in full force to occupy Afghanistan and to destroy al Qaeda's terrorist network. In early October 2001, "the U.S. launched air strikes against Afghanistan with cruise missiles, stealth bombers, Tomahawks, 'bunker-busting' missiles, and Mark 82 high drag bombs" (Roy 2002, 101). By late 2001, after nearly three months of massive U.S. air strikes, the Taliban and al Qaeda forces were destroyed or had fled to Pakistan.

Although fighting against terrorism was the proclaimed aim of the United States in rationalizing its invasion and occupation of Afghanistan, "there were other compelling reasons that drew U.S. power into Afghanistan": "The Central Asian region is rich in oil and gas reserves. The U.S. Department of Energy estimates that the Caspian basin holds 110 billion barrels, about three times the United States's own reserves. And Turkmenistan has immense natural gas supplies. Hence it should come as no surprise that U.S. policy elites were contemplating a military presence in Central Asia long before September 2001" (Parenti 2002b, 67).

"If one tries to make sense of the events that preceded or succeeded the terrorist attacks on the U.S.," writes Dimitris Yannopoulos in his article "Checkerboard of Oil, Minefields,"

> one need only "follow the money"—particularly the petrodollars. . . . It's all the money poised to cash in on the prospective oil bonanza of Central Asia. But there's also all the money set in motion to scuttle, delay or divert the most competitive and economically viable Eurasian pipeline plans.
>
> The stakes are therefore very high and key parameters can easily be lost in the logistical maze of the alternative Eurasian pipeline routes that already exist

around the Caspian Sea and those meant to expand, reroute or replace them. (2002, 51)

At the center of the competing oil pipeline projects lies the Central Asian Gas and Oil Pipelines project, which is planned "to transport oil and natural gas from Kazakhstan and Turkmenistan through Afghanistan and Pakistan all the way into India and the Arabian Sea. Each pipeline in this southbound route would be over 1,000 miles long, built at an estimated total project cost of $4.5 billion, with capacity to carry 700 billion cubic feet of gas and one million barrels of oil per day" (Yannopoulos 2002, 52).

"The discovery of vast oil and gas reserves in Kazakhstan and Turkmenistan," Parenti points out, "provided the lure, while the dissolution of the USSR removed the one major barrier against pursuing aggressive interventionist policy in that part of the world" (2000b, 67–68).

U.S. oil companies acquired the rights to some 75 percent of these new reserves. A major problem was how to extract the oil and gas from the landlocked region: U.S. officials opposed using the Russian pipeline or the most direct route across Iran to the Persian Gulf. Instead, they and the corporate oil contractors explored a number of alternative pipeline routes, across Azerbaijan and Turkey to the Mediterranean or across China to the Pacific. The one favored by Unocal, a US-based oil company, crossed Afghanistan and Pakistan to the Indian Ocean. The intensive negotiations that Unocal entered into with the Taliban regime were still unresolved by 1998, as an Argentine company placed a competing bid for the pipeline. Bush's war against the Taliban rekindled Unocal's hopes for getting a major piece of the action. (68)

According to Ted Rall in his article "The New Great Game: Oil Politics in Central Asia," Unocal's plan "is to extend Turkmenistan's existing system west to the Kazakh field on the Caspian and Southeast to the Pakistani port of Karachi on the Arabian Sea. That project runs through Afghanistan" (2002, 49). The significance of the U.S. intervention in Afghanistan, then, is more to its relationship to the country's strategic location with regard to the oil pipeline project that has been in the works for some time, than an immediate response to the September 11 events. As Parenti points out, what all these developments mean is that "the U.S. government had made preparations well in advance of September 2001 to move against the Taliban and create a compliant regime in Kabul and a direct U.S. military presence in Central Asia. The September 11 attacks provided the impetus, stampeding U.S. public opinion and reluctant allies into supporting military intervention" (2002b, 69).

Following the U.S. intervention in Afghanistan in late 2001, a compliant regime supportive of U.S. policy in Central Asia was installed to carry out U.S. military, geopolitical, and economic interests. Shortly thereafter, in June 2002 the Afghan government signed an agreement with Turkmenistan and Pakistan for the construction of an oil pipeline from Turkmenistan through Afghanistan and Pakistan to the Arabian Sea in order to transport oil from the Caspian Sea to the Pakistani port city of Karachi on the Arabian Sea. Thus was sealed the fate of Central Asian oil for the profits of the U.S. transnational oil companies who succeeded in expanding their area of control of this vital resource from the Middle East to the former Soviet territories in Central Asia—an expansion that facilitates their central role in furthering U.S. imperialist designs to dominate the world economy.

The Iraq War of 2003

In the aftermath of the war in Afghanistan and the drive to root out terrorism directed at the United States in the post-September 11 world, what the Bush Administration declared the "Axis of Evil"—a geopolitical area stretching from Iraq through Iran to North Korea—came to define the nature and direction of U.S. foreign policy toward the region, linking many of these states to the al Qaeda terrorist network.

The alleged links between Iraq and al Qaeda, implicating the Iraqi state in the September 11 attacks on the World Trade Center, provided the impetus to attack and disarm Iraq of "weapons of mass destruction" to prevent another terrorist act against the United States. Hence, with this argument, the United States tried to outmaneuver its long-time Western European allies by pushing for a United Nations resolution to declare war on Iraq through the U.N. Security Council. After failing to obtain the support of the council and threats of veto by France, Germany, and Russia, the United States and its coalition partners (primarily the British) launched a massive assault against Iraq by invading, bombing, and occupying Iraq in March 2003.

The ensuing "shock and awe" campaign of mass bombings launched several thousand tomahawk and cruise missiles against Iraqi targets, especially in Baghdad, including several presidential palaces, the Ministry of Information, command and control centers, and numerous other government buildings and bunkers. The bombings set the city ablaze for more than two weeks, causing much destruction and death. The U.S. and British troops engaged in bloody battles and met with stiff resistance from the Iraqi army, the Republican Guard, and irregulars, including the fedayeen and the paramilitary forces, who fought to defend Umm Qasr, Basra, An Nasiriyah, An Najaf, and Karbala, as well as Baghdad and other cities across Iraq. But by early April 2003, the U.S. forces succeeded in entering Baghdad, taking control of much of Iraq, and toppling the regime of Saddam Hussein.

The war against Iraq by the sole global superpower, the United States (and its imperialist junior partner, Britain), which unleashed hundreds of thousands of troops and several thousands of missiles and threatened the region with nuclear war, was designed to expand to include Syria and Iran in order to redraw the map of the entire Middle East region in favor of U.S. and Israeli interests. The aim was to lay claim to the oil resources of the Middle East by toppling the Baathist regimes in Iraq and Syria as well as the regime of the Ayatollahs in Iran, to neutralize the Arab opposition, and to crush the Palestinian movement in Gaza and the West Bank, so that a new U.S.-Israeli joint control over the region could be exerted, with efforts to colonize the area and to link it across the Fertile Crescent to the Caspian Sea and the Central Asian oil fields to Afghanistan and beyond. It is through this latest high-tech imperialist onslaught that the United States planned to impose its colossal rule over the region to reshape the new post–Cold War realities of the Middle East and the rest of the world—realities that have been shaping up within the framework of decades-long rivalries that have been taking place among the chief imperialist states for control of oil in the Middle East.

The Political Economy of Post–Cold War Realities in the Middle East

As the decades-long hostilities between the United States and the former Soviet Union in the Middle East have come to an end with the end of the Cold War, this important region of the world has reemerged as the arena for rivalries between the major capitalist powers of the world over sources of oil that is vital for their economies. Locked in interimperialist competition for control of raw materials, cheap labor, new markets, and higher rates of profit across the globe, the chief imperialist powers found in Iraq and Iran the potential for an alternate power center to control and regulate the flow of oil, which has become the key strategic commodity that will determine the success or failure of one or another of the rival capitalist powers in the world economy well into the twenty-first century.

Clearly, both Germany and Japan, and to a lesser extent other European powers like France, have been searching for a surrogate power in the Persian Gulf for over two decades. For a variety of reasons, including the financing of a decade-long war against Iran, Iraq became the power that could secure for Japan and Germany a future foothold in the Middle East, one that could eventually transfer Saudi power into Iraqi hands as a regional power broker for the two newly rising imperialist states. Decline in U.S. influence in the region in post-Shah and post-Saudi power politics and the rise of Germany and Japan through an expanding Iraqi hegemony over the Arabian Peninsula and the Persian Gulf could thus secure for German and Japanese capital direct access to sources of oil in the Middle East, bypassing the traditionally dominant position of the U.S. oil companies in the region.

This is exactly what happened in an earlier period of British imperial control over the Middle East, with U.S. encroachments to the region in direct rivalry to Britain's traditional hold over these territories, from Iran and Iraq to Jordan, Egypt, and down to the Arabian Peninsula including the entire Persian Gulf region. Now, in the same strategic territories a half century later, the same superpower rivals are involved in conflict once again, and for the very same reason: control of oil.

The disintegration of the Soviet Union as a military superpower, which during the postwar period played a key role in keeping in check U.S. encroachments throughout the world, allowed the United States to intervene in the Persian Gulf and succeed (at least for the time being) in outmaneuvering Germany and Japan, its archrivals, denying them direct access to sources of oil essential to their economic independence and emerging position in the world economy. Thus, the United States won, and its global rivals—Germany and Japan—wound up paying a substantial portion of the cost of an operation designed to suppress them.[10] The cost to Iraq was enormous in both human and material terms: over a hundred thousand Iraqi soldiers and thousands of innocent civilians were killed with billions of dollars' worth of destruction in a high-tech massacre inflicted on Iraq by the chief imperialist superpower, the United States.[11] A decade later, in 2001, the United States launched a similar military operation in Afghanistan that caused much devastation, destruction, and death, culminating with the overthrow of the Taliban regime and the installation of a government subservient to the United States.

With the latest U.S. war against Iraq in 2003 and the massive occupation of that country by several hundred thousand troops in order to topple the regime of Saddam Hussein, the United States became further entrenched in the Middle East, dominating the region by open military force.

Having been denied direct access to Middle Eastern oil, Germany, as the de facto leader of the European Union (EU), will play an increasingly central role within the EU and in relations with neighboring East European states extending to a number of the former Soviet republics, notably Russia and Ukraine, as it had with the former Soviet Union through the infamous German-Soviet natural gas pipeline agreement in the late 1980s.

As the European economy continues to grow and expand through increased commercial activity between member states, and as the EU becomes further consolidated through greater integration into a continental economic structure in which Germany continues to play a key role, the EU and its German nucleus will increasingly represent a viable challenge to U.S. power in the Middle East in the coming period.

Moreover, closer contact between Germany and Turkey to harness a long-standing relationship between the two countries, which goes back to the Ottoman period, may succeed in pulling Turkey away from the U.S. orbit in return for securing Turkish membership in the EU. This may also open access to the oil fields in eastern Turkey near the border with Iraq, and, through Turkey, extend Germany's influence to the latter's Central Asian ally, Azerbaijan, where Baku oil is exchanged for hard currency. Whichever of these possibilities become a reality, it is clear that a rising economic power such as Germany cannot for long pretend to be challenging the United States, while all along continuing to be dependent on it for its most vital source of raw material: oil.

Japan, on the other hand, has more limited but still quite plausible access to sources of oil in its part of the world. The most likely source is China, where Japan has already invested billions of dollars and enjoys a multiplicity of joint-venture benefits. China, as one of the world's largest producers of oil, would be eager to sell its excess capacity at levels below world market prices and still secure a steady source of guaranteed profits from its exports of this vital commodity to Japan and other rising capitalist economies in the region. Oil from Vietnam, Indonesia, and other Southeast Asian states, as well as from Siberia, could similarly fill an important part of Japanese demand and help Japan break loose from its dependence on the supply of Middle Eastern oil controlled by the U.S. oil monopolies.

With the United States remaining in firm control of the oil fields in the Middle East and further expanding its influence over Central Asia, Europe moving ahead with its full integration, and Japan continuing to expand its role and presence in the world economy, especially in the Pacific Rim, another clash of interests is bound to inflame as part of the long-standing rivalry between the chief competitors of the world economy in the early years of the twenty-first century. The U.S. war to disarm Iraq and to occupy its oil-rich territories in early 2003 is more related to this ongoing rivalry between the chief imperialist powers for control over oil in the Middle East, than the concern over the weapons of mass destruction that Iraq might still possess—weapons that were supplied to Iraq by the United States in the first place during the Iran-Iraq War in the 1980s.

For over two decades, since the overthrow of the Shah's regime in Iran in 1979, Iran and Iraq have been at the center of the rivalry between the chief imperialist states of the world capitalist system—the United States, Japan, Germany, and several other major European countries. As the long and bloody war between Iran and Iraq from 1980 to 1988 failed to fully resolve the power struggle between these rival regional powers in the Middle East, the United States became the chief arbiter in determining the balance of forces between these two rising states by first siding with Iran, then with Iraq, and finally against both. Japan, Germany, France, Italy, and other countries have in turn built a trading partnership by one or the other of these states locked in a power struggle challenging the traditional dominance of this region by Egypt and Saudi Arabia under the tutelage of U.S. imperialism.

The Persian Gulf War of 1991 became a test case of territorial control within the larger context of Middle Eastern geopolitics. The direct intervention of the United States in its war against Iraq in 1991 thus became the decisive response to the political turmoil that engulfed the region in the aftermath of the Cold War. The muscle flexed by the U.S. military machine in the Persian Gulf was thus meant to send a clear message to its imperialist archrivals that the United States continues to play a key role in the political economy of the Middle East. This role, which had been a dominant one throughout the post–World War II period, has once again been reestablished through the U.S. invasion of Afghanistan and by the U.S. war against Iraq in 2003 (as well as threats against other noncompliant states, like North Korea and Iran) culminating in new conflicts and destabilization of the world in the post-Soviet, post–Cold War "new world order" that now defines the parameters of great power politics in the Middle East and adjoining regions extending to Central Asia and beyond.

NOTES

1. Although economic rivalry between the major capitalist powers has intensified in recent years and surfaced as a major challenge to postwar U.S. hegemony over the world economy, the origins of such rivalry go back nearly a century, to when Britain, France, Germany, Japan, and the United States became part of the worldwide struggle for global supremacy—as manifested, for example, in the struggle over control of oil in the Middle East at the turn of the twentieth century—that later led to World War I. Today, in the post-Soviet environment, a similar struggle between the chief imperialist powers has extended the boundaries of this rivalry to lands beyond the greater Middle East, to the oil fields of the Caspian Sea and the surrounding countries of Central Asia.

2. It must be noted that a large percentage of these financial investments went to a single country, Bermuda.

3. The political implications of this shift away from raw materials investments and toward manufacturing investments are discussed at length by Berberoglu (1992b, chapter 3).

4. Nevertheless, in the 1970s and 1980s a growing number of Japanese corporations have been able to move part of their operations into the United States to supply the U.S. market from within, thus avoiding tariffs and other protectionist measures directed against them. Operating, in effect, as "American" corporations, some Japanese firms have thus escaped the problems associated with imports into the United States of goods manufactured abroad. The decline in U.S. wages relative to their increase in Japan during the past decade has been another important incentive for some Japanese firms to move part of their operations to the United States (Hook and Harukiyo 2001).

5. This, coupled with the possible long-term integration of Eastern Europe into the European Union, may indeed turn Europe into a rival economic superpower—one that has important political implications.

6. For varied explanations on the nature and causes of the Persian Gulf War of 1991, see Brenner (1991), Mayer (1991), Tanzer (1991), Headley (1991), Greer (1991), Berberoglu (1993).

7. According to a study by a University of New Hampshire economist Marc Herold, at least thirty-five hundred Afghan civilians died in U.S. bombing attacks between October 7 and December 6, 2001. See Herold (2002, 116).

8. For this, the United States paid off the Taliban in a big way. According to Ted Rall's November 2, 2001, *San Francisco Chronicle* report cited by Parenti, "as recently as 1999, the U.S. government paid the entire annual salary of every single Taliban government official" (2002b, 64).

9. The lead headline of the August 12, 2002, issue of *Time* magazine, which devoted its cover story to a "Special Report: The Secret History—They Had a Plan" of the Afghan war, reads, "Nine months before 9/11 the U.S. had a bold plan to attack al-Qaeda. It wasn't carried out until the towers fell." See Elliott (2002, 28–43).

10. Japan was made to pay $13 billion and Germany $10 billion as part of "their share" of the cost of the war to secure U.S. victory! See Knowlton and Rapoport (1991, 58).

11. See the *New York Times* (March 28, 1991) for a transcript of General Norman Schwarzkopf's interview "Talking with David Frost," in which the general said, "I would estimate . . . that we easily killed more than 100,000 [Iraqi soldiers]" (quoted in Greer 1991, 3).

Chapter Six

The Imperial State and Control of the Global Political Economy

Since the end of the nineteenth century, the modern state in advanced capitalist societies has evolved parallel to the centralization of the capitalist economy in its transition to the higher, monopoly stage. In line with its role in facilitating the existing mode of production and its attendant superstructure, the political apparatus of modern capitalism has come to reflect the changing structure of the capitalist economy, which increasingly operates on a global level. With the globalization of capital, the leading capitalist state of the advanced capitalist economies has come to assume a greater responsibility in organizing and leading the global capitalist system, thus adopting the role of an imperial state charged with the control and rationalization of the global political economy (Beams 1998; Halliday 2001). It is within this context of the worldwide expansion of the advanced capitalist superstructure that the crisis of the imperial state manifests itself on a global scale.[1]

This chapter examines the role of the imperial state in the context of the global capitalist economy, where the globalization of capital—through the worldwide expansion of transnational monopolies—has had a decisive effect on the role and functions of the capitalist state and brought to the fore new and more pervasive contradictions, leading to a crisis of management and legitimacy of capitalism on a worldwide basis. It is argued that this has been the result of developments in the latest stage of capitalist expansion, in which the monopoly fraction of the capitalist class in the advanced capitalist countries, especially the United States, has secured a thorough control of the state apparatus to advance fully its interests at home and abroad and has succeeded in blocking the state from fulfilling its role in advancing the broader, long-term interests of capitalism and the capitalist class as a whole.

Debates on the nature and role of the imperial state in the global political economy over the past two decades have contributed much to our understanding of the conflicts and contradictions arising within the modern capitalist state as an outcome of the changing balance of forces, both within the economy and the state apparatus itself.[2] Despite the arguments of some critics to the contrary, what emerged from these debates is the understanding that in the advanced, monopoly stage of capitalism, the capitalist state no longer represents the varied fractional interests of the capitalist class as a whole, as was the case in the early twentieth century prior to the rise of the monopolies and the monopoly fraction of the capitalist class (Szymanski 1978; Parenti 2002a).[3]

As capitalism developed from its competitive to monopoly (imperialist) stage, the state increasingly lost its "relative autonomy" vis-à-vis the various fractions of the capitalist class and became an agent to safeguard and advance the interests of its most powerful fraction: monopoly capital. This has been the case in Europe since the 1880s, and in the United States since the early 1900s, especially since World War II (Perlo 1988). During this period, the monopolies in the advanced capitalist countries have become so powerful, through both national and global economic expansion, that the protection and further advancement of their immense economic wealth at home and abroad has resulted in their outright control of the state apparatus at every conceivable level. The political crisis resulting from this fractional domination and fragmentation has led to a crisis of the advanced-capitalist imperial state, especially its current global leading force, the U.S. imperial state.

THE CRISIS OF THE U.S. STATE
AS THE LEADING IMPERIAL STATE

While the changes at work in the U.S. economy and society have their roots in earlier decades when the consolidation of U.S. monopoly power began to take hold on a world scale, the increased globalization of U.S. capital under the auspices of U.S. transnational monopolies in recent decades has affected various classes and segments of U.S. society unevenly. The diverse impact of economic changes during this period on different classes and fractions of classes are precipitating causes of the unfolding political crisis of the capitalist state in the United States. In this context, the intensified globalization of U.S. capital and the decline of the U.S. domestic economy since the early 1970s constitute the material basis of the crisis of the advanced capitalist state in the United States during the past three decades (Phillips 1998; Brecher and Costello 1998).

The period from 1945 to the present saw an unparalleled growth of U.S. transnational capital throughout the world, but the postwar boom that reached its peak during the Vietnam War came to an abrupt end when the U.S. defeat in Southeast Asia (which brought to a halt major war contracts to U.S. corporations) plunged the economy into a severe recession by the mid-1970s. So powerful was the impact of its defeat in Vietnam that the United States has been unable to alter the situation in any fundamental way. As a result, the decline of U.S. global hegemony has become irreversible.

Given the logic of capital accumulation on a world scale in late capitalist society, it is no accident that the decline of the U.S. domestic economy since the early 1970s corresponds to the accelerated export of U.S. capital abroad in search of cheap labor, access to raw materials, new markets, and higher rates of profit. The resulting deindustrialization of the U.S. economy in the final decades of the twentieth century has had a serious impact on workers and other affected segments of the laboring population and has brought about a major dislocation of the domestic economy (Bluestone and Harrison 1982; Berberoglu 1992a; Phillips 1998). This has necessitated further state intervention on behalf of the monopolies and has heightened the contradictions that led to the crisis of the U.S. state.

The crisis of the advanced capitalist state in the United States manifests itself at different levels, ranging from international conflicts (interimperialist rivalry, disintegration of regional political and military alliances, and the inability to suppress nationalist movements and revolution in the Third World), to domestic economic problems (trade and budget deficits, monetary and fiscal crisis, unemployment, recession, and so on), to national political crisis (factional struggles within the capitalist class, problems of legitimacy, repression of the working class and mass movements, militarization of the polity and society, and so on) (Perlo 1988; Parenti 2002a).[4]

The most critical problem facing the U.S. state as the leading imperial state, however, is the crisis emanating from the restructuring of the international division of labor involving plant closings and the transfer of the production process to overseas territories. The consequent deindustrialization in the imperial center has led to higher unemployment and underemployment, pressing down wages to minimum levels in the United States (Bluestone and Harrison 1982; Perlo 1988),[5] while imperial-installed puppet regimes have intensified the repression of workers and peasants in the Third World and forced on them starvation wages in order to generate superprofits for the U.S. monopolies (Ross 1997; Roy 1999).

WORLDWIDE CONTRADICTIONS
AND CRISIS OF THE IMPERIAL STATE

The crisis of the imperial state on the global scene is a manifestation of the contradictions of the world economy, which in the early twenty-first century has reached a critical stage in its development. The massive flow of U.S. transnational investment throughout the world, especially in Western Europe, Japan, and other advanced capitalist regions, has led to the post–World War II reemergence of interimperialist rivalry between the major capitalist powers, while fostering antagonisms between them in the scramble for the peripheral regions of the global capitalist economy—Latin America, Asia, Africa, and the Middle East (Hart 1992; Falk 1999; Halliday 2001).

With the integration of the economies of Western Europe into the European Union (EU) and the emergence of Japan as a powerful economic force, the position of the United States in the global economy has declined relative to both its own postwar supremacy in the 1940s and 1950s and to other advanced capitalist economies since that time. Despite the fact that U.S. capital continues to control the biggest share of overseas markets and accounts for the largest volume of international investments, its hold on the global economy has recently begun slipping in a manner similar to Britain's in the early twentieth century. This has, in turn, led the U.S. state to take a more aggressive role in foreign policy to protect U.S. transnational interests abroad. Its massive deployment in the Middle East in the early 1990s, which led to the Persian Gulf War of 1991, and most recently its intervention in Afghanistan in 2001 and war against Iraq in 2003, has resulted in great military expenditures and translated into an enormous burden on working people of the United States, who have come to shoulder the colossal cost of maintaining a global empire whose vast military machine encompasses the world.

In the current phase of the crisis of the U.S. imperial state, the problems it faces are of such magnitude that they threaten the very existence of the global capitalist system as a global power bloc. Internal economic and budgetary problems have been compounded by ever-growing military spending propped up by armed intervention in the Third World (Grenada, Panama, Iraq, Afghanistan, and so on), while a declining economic base at home manifested in the banking crisis, deindustrialization, and a recessionary economy further complicated by the global rivalry between the major capitalist powers that is not always restricted to the economic field, but has political (and even military) implications that are global in magnitude (Beams 1998).

The growing prospects of interimperialist rivalry between the major capitalist powers, backed up by their states, are effecting changes in their relations that render the global political economy an increasingly unstable character. Competition between the United States, Japan, and European imperial states representing the interests of their own respective capitalist classes are leading them on a collision course for world supremacy, manifested in struggles for markets, raw materials, and spheres of influence in geopolitical—as well as economic—terms, which may in fact lead to a new balance of forces, and consequently alliances that will have serious political implications in global power politics. As the continuing economic ascendence of the major capitalist rivals of the United States take their prominent position in the global economy, pressures will build toward the politicization and militarization of these states from within, where the leading class forces bent on dominating the world economy will press forward with the necessary political and military corollary of their growing economic power in the global capitalist system (Hart 1992; Falk 1999), as has been the case with the German and French position against war with Iraq on the U.N. Security Council in 2003.

These developments in global economic and geopolitical shifts in the balance of forces among the major capitalist powers will bring to the fore new and yet untested international alliances for world supremacy and domination in the post–Cold War era. Such alliances will bring key powers like Russia and China into play in a new and complicated relationship that holds the key for the success or failure of the new rising imperial centers that will emerge as the decisive forces in the global economic, political, and military equation in the early twenty-first century (Halliday 2001).

The contradictions and conflicts imbedded in relations between the rival states of the major capitalist powers will again surface as an important component of international relations in the years ahead. And these are part and parcel of the restructuring of the international division of labor and the transfer of production to overseas territories in line with the globalization of capital on a worldwide basis—a process that has serious consequences for the economies of both the advanced capitalist and less developed countries. Economic decline in the imperial centers (manifested in plant closings, unemployment, and recession) and superexploitation of workers in the Third World (maintained by repressive military regimes) yield the same combined result that has a singular global logic: the accumulation of transnational profits for the capitalist class of the advanced capitalist countries—above all, that of the United States, the current center of global capitalism. It is in this context of the changes that are taking place on a world scale that the imperial state is beginning to confront the current crisis of global capitalism.

The contradictions of the unfolding process of global expansion and accumulation have brought to the fore new political realities: renewed repression at home and abroad to control an increasingly frustrated working class in the imperial heartland, and a militant and revolutionary mass of workers and peasants in the neocolonial states of the Third World poised to resist capitalist globalization (Houtart and Polet 2001). It is these inherent contradictions of modern monopoly capital that are making it increasingly difficult for the imperial state to control and manage the global political economy, while at the same time preparing the conditions for international solidarity of workers on a world scale.

CRISIS OF THE CAPITALIST STATE IN THE THIRD WORLD

The expansion of monopoly capital to the Third World has been accompanied by the rise of the authoritarian state, especially in those formations critical to the profit needs of the transnational corporations. Thus, Brazil, Argentina, Chile, the Philippines, South Korea, Taiwan, Indonesia, Iran, and Turkey, among others, have all experienced the domination of a rightist authoritarian state, often in the form of a neofascist military dictatorship, albeit installed to power by the imperialist forces outside the state's geographic boundaries (Petras and Veltmeyer 2001).[6]

The rise to power of right-wing repressive states in the Third World are a by-product of imperialism in its late capitalist stage, which finds itself in a position where its domination can be ensured only through brute military force. This is accomplished through the installation of repressive military dictatorships in some countries and—what amounts to the same thing—the installation of right-wing "civilian" authoritarian regimes that violate the most basic human rights of the people. Here, the role of the key institutions of the imperial state—from "intelligence" agencies to paramilitary units—become the decisive forces that subvert the internal political institutions of Third World states in order to maintain imperial control over the authoritarian regimes installed into power and to eliminate popular opposition to their rule (Parenti 1995). In this way, the repressive state in the Third World becomes an appendage of the imperial state and operates in accordance with its dictates. It is in this sense that the crisis of the imperial state at the global level translates into a crisis of the capitalist state in the Third World.

With the growth of foreign investment and economic activity in a growing number of Third World countries, there has been a marked increase in the number and strength of the working class, leading to strikes, demonstrations, and open defiance of the repressive neocolonial capitalist state (Munck 2002).

This, in turn, has led to further repression of the masses, while at the same time plunging the state into a deep crisis of legitimacy where order is maintained through the brute force of the army and the police. Such repression has, in turn, led to a further crisis of the authoritarian state and elevated the class struggle to a higher level, at which the masses have succeeded in overthrowing these regimes in a number of countries around the world, including Iran, Nicaragua, the Philippines, Argentina, Brazil, and Chile. Added to their economic bankruptcy through a mounting foreign debt, double- and triple-digit inflation, and alarming rates of unemployment, the political crisis of the capitalist state in these Third World formations, which has led to military/police repression, has thus fueled the forces of change and revolution (Waterman 1998; Smith and Johnston 2002).

The logic of transnational capitalist expansion on a global scale is such that it leads to the emergence and development of forces in conflict with this expansion. The working class has been in the forefront of these forces; strikes, mass demonstrations, political organizing through party formation, confrontation with the local client state machine, armed insurrection, civil war, and revolutionary upheavals are all part and parcel of the contradictory structure of relations imposed on the laboring people throughout the world by transnational capital, the imperial state, and its client states in the Third World.

RESPONSES TO THE CRISIS OF THE CAPITALIST STATE ON A GLOBAL SCALE

The worldwide expansion of global capital during the course of the twentieth century, especially since World War II, has led to struggles between labor and capital on a world scale, particularly in regions and countries of the world where global capital has made the greatest headway.

In Latin America, these are the relatively more developed and larger countries of Brazil, Mexico, and Argentina, and increasingly Peru, Chile, and a number of countries in Central America and the Caribbean region. These struggles, in the form of strikes, demonstrations, mass protests, and a variety of direct and indirect political actions, have intensified in recent years, especially in Argentina.

The strong presence of Western, especially U.S., dominance in Asia over a long span of time has prompted a wave of uprisings in recent decades, from Indonesia to Thailand, to Burma, to South Korea, to the Philippines. Working people of Asia have struggled for decades to improve their condition and to protect their interests, and in so doing confronting the powers of the repressive state.

In Africa, too, class struggles are unfolding with exceptional speed. The popular forces fighting for national liberation and social revolution are waging a determined struggle to break loose from the neocolonial bondage chained to the transnational monopolies and the imperial state. From Morocco and Tunisia in the north, to Kenya and Uganda in the east, to Ghana and Nigeria in the west, to South Africa, workers and the oppressed have risen to take charge of their own destinies. Inspired by the victory of the revolutions in Angola, Mozambique, and Zimbabwe, and the struggle against apartheid in South Africa, the African masses are fighting to liberate themselves from imperialism and neocolonialism throughout the continent.

The development of capitalism in the Middle East, both in its neocolonial and state-capitalist forms, has engendered intensified class conflicts and struggles throughout the region in recent decades. Working-class and popular struggles have intensified in Egypt, Turkey, Iran, and the Persian Gulf states. The crisis in the Persian Gulf, which unleashed the forces of U.S. imperialism into the region, further fueled the discontent of the masses. The U.S. intervention in Afghanistan in 2001, the second Palestinian intifada from 2000 to 2002, and the U.S. war against Iraq in 2003 have further enflamed the growing mass opposition to U.S. imperialist encroachments into the region in recent years.

In the heartland of imperialism—Europe and the United States—millions of workers affected by plant closings and the depression in the auto, steel, electronics, telecommunications, and other related industries have taken militant actions against the corporate offensive. Thus, increasingly politicized strikes and demonstrations by U.S. and European workers have been on the rise during the past decade.

Although strikes, protests, and other forms of defiance in and of themselves may not always lead to major political changes in a given country, they may nevertheless be viewed as a necessary first step in advancing the subjective conditions toward greater radicalization and class consciousness among workers, setting the stage for deeper and more lasting social transformations that may follow at a later date. Given the politicized nature of the prevailing economy and social conditions in Latin America and much of Asia, Africa, and the Middle East, as well as parts of Western Europe and, increasingly, the United States, strike actions by organized labor for what seems at first purely economic gains may soon (as has often been the case) turn into political protest against the government, local ruling classes, and imperialism, raising issues far beyond wages and working conditions toward political action to alter the existing neocolonial capitalist order.

When we consider the totality of the political forces at work in the Third World, together with those in Europe and other advanced capitalist regions, including the United States, it is clear that the potential unity of the working class and other laboring sections of society across national boundaries is much closer to the reality of the unfolding process at work throughout the world than has been the case until recently. The material conditions that have led to U.S. imperial domination of the global economy up to the present period have now reached a point where broad segments of the masses the world over, under working-class leadership, are coming together to challenge it at its very foundations.

If the logic of imperialist expansion is capitalist domination of the world, and if the imperial state is unable to control and contain the growing contradictions of the global capitalist economy, then the process of capitalist exploitation on a world scale is preparing the eventual rise of the working class in the struggle over control of the capitalist state throughout the world.

NOTES

1. For a detailed discussion of the political implications of the globalization of capital for the capitalist state and its role in the world economy, see Berberoglu (1987b, 1992b, 2001).

2. For a summary of the various major positions on the theory of the state debated in the 1970s and 1980s, see Berberoglu (2001, chapter 2); see also Gold, Lo, and Wright (1985) and Szymanski (1978, 21–31, and chapters 6–11), as well as the works of Ralph Miliband, Nicos Poulantzas, Claus Offe, and the *Kapitalistate* collective.

3. For an analysis of positions contrary to this view, see Esping-Andersen, Friedland, and Wright (1976) and Block (1977, 1978). These authors maintain that the capitalist state continues to be "relatively autonomous" of the capitalist class, despite the disproportionately favorable position of the monopolies within the economy and society. For a critique of such arguments, see Berberoglu (2001, 36–48).

4. For a discussion of various aspects of the crisis in the 1980s, see O'Connor (1973), Mandel (1980), Perlo (1988). For an analysis of the situation in the 1990s and beyond, see Brecher and Costello (1998).

5. See also Sherman (1976), Devine (1982), and Harrison and Bluestone (1988).

6. For early corporatist interpretations of the Third World state, see Stepan (1978). On bureaucratic authoritarianism, see O'Donnell (1973, 1979). On the neofascist character of the dependent states ruled by military dictatorships, see Petras (1981, chapters 7 and 10). For a discussion on the nature of the bureaucratic authoritarian and other forms of the dependent state, see Berberoglu (1987b, chapter 7; 2001, chapter 6); see also Carnoy (1984, chapter 7).

Chapter Seven

Global Capitalist Expansion and Domestic Economic Decline in the United States

The globalization of U.S. capital and the restructuring of the international division of labor during the past three decades has plunged the U.S. economy into crisis in a contradictory way: the superprofits obtained from corporate takeovers and acquisitions resulting from the bull market and the megamergers of the 1980s and the 1990s have been accompanied by record business bankruptcies, bank failures, the savings and loan crisis, huge trade and budget deficits, declining real wages, and a widening gap between the wealthy and the working class. However, the October 1987 stock market crash, the $500 billion savings and loan disaster in 1989–1991, and, more recently, the collapse of the Trump empire and the latest Enron and WorldCom scandals in 2001–2002 have shown the limits of capital accumulation through frenzied speculative financial activity, accounting scams, and empire building on the backs of the working people who have called into question the legitimacy of the capitalist system.

As the drive for bigger profits has resulted in large-scale plant closings in the United States and the transfer of the production process to overseas territories, the consequent deindustrialization has led to higher unemployment and underemployment in the United States, pressing down wages to minimum levels (see Harrison and Bluestone 1988; Phillips 1998). The contradictions of this process of worldwide expansion and accumulation have brought to the fore new realities of capitalist economics, now characterized by industrial decline and class polarization, accompanied by a renewed assault on the living standards of millions of working people in the United States, while a small minority of the corporate rich continues to accumulate great wealth and fortunes from the ever-growing expansion of capitalism on a world scale.

DECLINE OF THE U.S. ECONOMY
IN RECENT DECADES

A number of factors have brought about the decline of the U.S. economy during the past three decades: the ending of the Vietnam War, the oil crisis, the
rise to world prominence of European and Japanese economies (i.e., interimperialist rivalry), the effects of the globalization of U.S. capital on the U.S.
economy, and problems associated with the capitalist business cycle leading
to periodic recessions. These, combined with the structural transformation of
the U.S. economy in line with its role in the new international division of labor, brought forth in 1974–1975 the most severe economic downturn since
the 1930s (Mandel 1980; Sherman 1976). The gravity of the situation in the
mid-1970s was such that the post-1975 recovery could not sustain itself for
more than a few years, then sank the economy into another recession in
1979–1980 and a much deeper one in 1982, then again another in 1992, followed by yet another in 2001–2003.

While short-term government policies since 1983 have managed to regulate symptoms of the underlying structural defects in the economy and post-
poned the crisis, the expected big decline in the stock market in the coming
period may prove to be much worse than any such decline previously, for
the cumulative impact of the developing capitalist crisis is destined to bring
the world economy to a head, especially in its nucleus, the United States.
The highly speculative nature of the stock market in the 1990s (a situation
similar to that of the 1920s) points to such an outcome as a likely development in the early years of the twenty-first century as evidenced by the sharp
drop in the value of the National Association of Securities Dealers Auto-
matic Quotations (NASDAQ) stocks from their highs in 2000 to their
lowest levels in 2002.[1] Decline in capacity utilization in manufacturing industry, record trade deficits, growing unemployment, decline in real wages
and purchasing power, small business bankruptcies and farm foreclosures,
bank failures, a shaky international financial system, record government
deficits, and a highly speculative stock market are grave symptoms of a declining national economy following a decade-long bull market in the 1990s
that led to record corporate profits, megamergers, and wholesale acquisitions and takeovers that favorably affected the biggest U.S. corporations.[2]

In examining the data for the 1970s, 1980s, and 1990s, we find that the
continued overproduction of goods in manufacturing and other industries has
resulted in ever-larger inventories. During this period, manufacturing inventories more than quadrupled, rising from $102 billion in 1970, to $265 billion
in 1980, to $405 billion in 1990, to $492 billion in 2000 (U.S. Council of Eco-

nomic Advisers 1990, 314, 358; 2001, 341). Similarly, such increases in other sectors of the economy led to a sharp rise in total inventories, from $179 billion in 1970, to $509 billion in 1980, to $841 billion in 1990, to $1.2 trillion in 2000 (U.S. Department of Commerce 1991, 15, S-5; U.S. Council of Economic Advisers 1990, 314, 358; 2001, 340). This, in turn, has impacted total output, such that cutbacks in production have resulted in a reduction in capacity utilization in manufacturing, which fell from 89.5 percent in 1965 to 77 percent in 1971, to 72 percent in 1975, to 70 percent in 1982, during the three consecutive recessions of the 1970s and early 1980s. The decline in durable goods production was even more pronounced as it fell from 87 percent in 1967, to 73 percent in 1971, to 70 percent in 1975, to 67 percent in 1982 (Council of Economic Advisers 1989, 365). Similarly, there was a sharp decline in net private domestic investment during the 1975 and 1982 recessions, falling from $257 billion in 1973 to $96 billion in 1975, and from $253 billion in 1978 to $64 billion in 1982 (327). The ups and downs of the business cycle over this period show that the general trend in business activity has been in a downward direction, with each peak lower than the one that preceded it and each trough deeper and worse than what came before.

While the decade of the 1990s has been characterized as a period of economic boom, largely because of the tremendous rise in stock prices through widespread speculation in the stock market, especially in high-tech and internet stocks, other vital indicators have shown the general weakness of the U.S. economy. Thus, while capacity utilization in manufacturing industry stood at 84 percent in 1989, it fell to 82 percent in 1990, to 78 percent in 1991, climbed to 82 percent by 1994, and remained around 81 to 82 percent during the second half of the 1990s. The decline in durable goods production has been even sharper with a drop in capacity utilization from 82 percent in 1989, to 79 percent in 1990, to 75 percent in 1991, and remaining around 81 percent during the second half of the 1990s (U.S. Council of Economic Advisers 2001, 337). With the onset of the latest recession in 2001, however, the U.S. economy has once again begun to move in a downward direction.

Looking at the international trade situation, one can observe that the intensified overseas expansion of U.S. transnational corporations has had a serious impact on the U.S. export-import structure, resulting in large trade deficits. This came about as a result of a continuous drop in U.S. exports due to plant closings and a sharp increase in imports from overseas subsidiaries of U.S. transnationals.[3]

Since the mid-1970s, the U.S. trade deficit has greatly increased, reaching $25 billion in 1980, $109 billion in 1990, and $452 billion in 2000 (U.S. Council of Economic Advisers 2001, 392). While U.S. transnational expansion abroad continued with exceptional speed during the 1970s, it took on a new significance by the early 1980s, as imports into the United States of manufactured goods produced by U.S. transnational subsidiaries overseas started to affect the U.S. trade balance in a consistently negative direction beginning in 1982. Thus, as imports of manufactured goods increased from $186 billion in 1982, to $436 billion in 1990, to over $1 trillion in 2000, the trade deficit for manufactured goods increased from $12 billion in 1982, to $87 billion in 1990, to $384 billion in 2000 (U.S. Council of Economic Advisers 2001, 392). Although foreign imports are partly responsible for the shift in the balance of U.S. merchandise trade in manufactured goods, increasing penetration of the Japanese and European economies by U.S. transnationals has led to the acquisition of a growing percentage of the stocks of foreign competitors in their home territories (Bluestone and Harrison 1982). For example, General Motors has substantial control of Isuzu, Chrysler owns a large share of Mitsubishi, and Ford has a controlling interest in Mazda. There is a similar move by these and other U.S. corporations to take over some of the largest firms in South Korea, such as Samsung. This new development, together with the transfer of productive facilities of U.S.-based transnational monopolies to cheap labor areas overseas, coupled with the expansion of low-cost, subcontracted exports from China, not "unfair competition" by foreign companies, explains in large part the record U.S. trade deficit in recent years.

Another major problem endemic to the present U.S. political economy is the budget deficit. As an extension of postwar Keynesian "remedies" to recessions and depressions brought about by the capitalist business cycle, government spending has led to an enormous growth in the national debt over the past three decades. The situation worsened during the 1980s when a huge increase in military spending combined with a large tax cut for business resulted in record annual budget deficits, vastly increasing the total government debt and the interest paid on the debt (Magdoff and Sweezy 1987). As military spending more than doubled since 1980 and more than tripled since the mid-1970s (rising above $300 billion in the 1990s), the gross federal debt increased immensely, from $909 billion in 1980, to $3.2 trillion in 1990, to $5.6 trillion in 2000, while the net interest paid on the debt rose from $59 billion in 1980, to $211 billion in 1990, to $261 billion in 2000 (Council of Economic Advisers 2001, 367, 373).

This vast amount of government spending, especially on the military and the interest paid on the debt, together with an expanded consumer credit system now over $10 trillion, has thus far averted the collapse of the U.S. economy. The widening gap between the accumulated wealth of the capitalist class and the declining incomes of workers and the self-employed (within a deteriorating national economy and the state's budgetary crisis) has led to a political crisis within the state apparatus and has sharpened the class struggle.

THE IMPACT OF THE ECONOMIC
DECLINE ON THE WORKING CLASS

One consequence of the transfer of the production process to low-wage Third World countries has been a proportionate decline in the U.S. manufacturing workforce relative to the total labor force and a commensurate increase in the proportion of low-paid labor in the service sector. Thus, between 1970 and 2000 the proportion of workers in goods-producing industries declined from 33.3 percent of the labor force in 1970, to 28.4 percent in 1980, to 22.7 percent in 1990, to 19.5 percent in 2000; in the manufacturing industry, it dropped from 27.3 percent in 1970, to 22.4 percent in 1980, to 17.4 percent in 1990, to 13.9 percent in 2000 (U.S. Council of Economic Advisers 2001, 328). On the other hand, a segment of the unemployed manufacturing workforce that was able to obtain employment in the low-paid service sector accelerated the growth of this sector during the past two decades, such that the proportion of workers in this sector, relative to the total labor force, increased from 66.7 percent in 1970, to 71.6 percent in 1980, to 77.2 percent in 1990, to 80.5 percent in 2000 (329).

As the economy has been unable to generate sufficient employment relative to the growth of the labor force in general, there has been a steady increase in the rate of unemployment during this period. And in line with the general trends in the economy over the previous three decades, the unemployment rate has also become a broad indicator of the direction and severity of the economic decline and its impact on the working class in the United States: its rate was 5.9 percent during the 1971 recession, 8.5 percent during the 1975 recession, 9.7 percent during the 1982 recession, and 7.5 percent during the 1992 recession (Council of Economic Advisers 2001, 325). Black unemployment has followed an identical pattern, but at a much higher level: it was 10.4 percent in 1972, 14.8 percent in 1975, 18.9 percent in 1982, and 14.2 percent in 1992 (U.S. Department of Commerce 1991, S-10; U.S. Council of Economic Advisers 1990, 339; 2001, 325). This pattern of double unemployment rate for blacks continued to prevail during the latest recession beginning in 2001. Thus, while deep into the recession in December 2002 total unemployment had reached 6.0 percent, black unemployment had climbed to 11.5 percent (U.S. Department of Labor 2003, table A-2).

Inflation is another factor that negatively impacts the economic position of those dependent on wages and fixed incomes. As U.S. capitalism has developed from its competitive to monopoly stage during the past one hundred years and established itself as the dominant force within the world economy following World War II, inflation has become a permanent feature of the U.S. economy, rising at a steady pace during the past several decades (Sherman 1976). Thus, while the peaks in price rises during the earlier stages of capitalist development in the United States occurred during periods of war—the Civil War, World War I, and World War II—and were caused mainly by government spending on the military that necessitated the excess printing of money to pay for war-related expenditures, the post-1945 rise in the inflation rate, which in good part was fueled by the Korean and Vietnam Wars, was mainly effected by the rise to power of monopoly capital that could (and did) raise prices at will, without the constraint of competitive forces in the market—forces that had kept prices in check at an earlier, premonopoly stage.

With the monopoly structure of the economy in place and in full force, vertically integrated large corporations, controlling key sectors of the production, marketing, and distribution network, were able to exert their power and fix prices at ever higher levels (Sherman 1976). Thus, between the mid-1960s and late 1980s prices rose by more than 300 percent. Most of this increase occurred beginning in the 1970s, when the giant monopolies came to consolidate their position in the economy. During the first half of the 1970s, the rate of inflation averaged 7 percent per year; during the second half of the 1970s, it averaged 9 percent per year, reaching a high of 13.5 percent in 1980 (U.S. Department of Commerce 1988, 385; U.S. Council of Economic Advisers 1991, 336, 355).[4]

With increasing unemployment and spiraling inflation during the 1970s and early 1980s, real wages of workers continued to decline during this period, registering a drop of 7.2 percent from 1974 to 1975 and nearly 12 percent from 1979 to 1982; from 1974 to 1995, U.S. workers showed a net loss of 20 percent in their real income (U.S. Department of Commerce 1988, 385; U.S. Council of Economic Advisers 1991, 336, 355). While the situation improved a bit during the late 1990s, when workers were able to gain 6.3 percent in real wages, the recession that began in 2001 once again forced real wages in a downward direction.

The persistence of income inequality between working men and women during this period made matters worse for women workers, whose income continued to register a big gap in comparison with men's wages, thus perpetuating the added exploitation of women at rates much higher than men. A similar gap in income between white and nonwhite workers became worse by the racist offensive of the 1980s (Melendez 1988, 12–15).

The general decline in real wages and the continuing race and gender income gap since the mid-1970s, however, has led to a decline in purchasing power and living standard of U.S. workers over the past three decades, such that in 1999, the purchasing power of the dollar, as measured by consumer prices in 1982–1984 dollars, declined to its lowest level in thirty years to sixty cents (U.S. Department of Commerce 2000, 485).

INCREASING CLASS POLARIZATION

A key factor in the decline in purchasing power and living standard for workers in the United States has been a rise in the rate of surplus value (or exploitation) and a consequent drop in labor's share over the years (Perlo 1988, 35–54). Thus, while both production and productivity per labor hour increased continuously during the postwar period, labor's share drastically fell from 40 percent in 1950 to 25 percent in 1984; at the same time, the rate of surplus value in U.S. manufacturing industry more than doubled from 150 percent in 1950 to 302 percent in 1984 (512). By 1999, the rate of surplus value in manufacturing industry had climbed to 451 percent, and labor's share dropped to 18 percent (U.S. Bureau of the Census 2001, 620). This, together with favorable government policies toward large corporations (e.g., capital gains tax cuts), has resulted in record corporate profits. Looking at the past two decades, we find that total net corporate profits more than quadrupled, from $209 billion in 1980, to $389 billion in 1990, to over $900 billion in 2000 (U.S. Council of Economic Advisers 2001, 380). Likewise, profits of domestic industries increased severalfold during this period, mostly accounted for by nonfinancial industries. Even taking inflation into account—it has been quite low in the 1980s and 1990s—net corporate profits have surged during this period, more than doubling in real terms.[5]

To obtain a more accurate picture of the situation and be able to calculate the rate of surplus value, however, we need to look at gross profits, for net profits hide the amount of total value created by workers that has already been distributed to other segments of the nonlaboring population, such as in the case of corporate executive salaries and federal, state, and local government taxes, and to numerous other industries and commercial enterprises. All these deducted business expenses are paid for from the total amount of value created by workers.

An examination of the extent of concentration and centralization of capital, which reveals the extent of monopolization of the economy and thereby the degree of polarization between social classes, indicates that in 1999 some six hundred manufacturing corporations, each with assets of $1 billion or more, had combined assets of $3.3 trillion and a net profit of $209 billion, and accounted for 77.6 percent of all manufacturing assets and 80.2 percent of total net profits (U.S. Bureau of the Census 2000, 558).[6]

While immense wealth has been accumulating in the hands of the wealthy owners of the giant corporations during this period of economic decline and crises, more and more workers have been experiencing a sharp drop in their real wages and standard of living over the past three decades. The resultant growing polarization between labor and capital has thus become crystallized in the distribution of income and wealth in the United States (Braun 1991; Kloby 1991; Rothman 2002).

This is evident in data on the distribution of income in the United States over the past three decades. Thus, between 1970 and 2000, while the share in total income of the top 5 percent and the highest fifth of families increased, the share of the bottom three-fifths of families decreased. Data on the concentration of wealth in the United States also show the widening gap between the wealthy and the working class in recent decades. Thus, according to available data, between 1963 and 1983 the richest 10 percent of families have increased their share of total wealth by nearly 7 percent, owning by 1983 nearly 72 percent of all assets, and the top 0.5 percent of families have increased their share by nearly 10 percent, owning 35 percent of all assets, while the remaining 90 percent of families have experienced a drop in their share of total wealth by nearly 7 percent (Kloby 1987, 7). Moreover, if we exclude from these data homes for personal use, the disparity in wealth becomes even more glaring: in 1983, the richest 10 percent of families owned over 83 percent of all assets and the top 0.5 percent of families owned nearly half of all assets, while the remaining 90 percent of families owned less than 17 percent of the total. Furthermore, the richest 10 percent of families owned 78 percent of real estate, 89 percent of corporate stock, over 90 percent of bonds, and nearly 94 percent of all business assets. More significantly, the top 0.5 percent of all families accounted for nearly or over half of all assets, corporate stock, bonds, and business assets (Joint Economic Committee of the U.S. Congress cited in Kloby 1987, 4–6; 1993, 30–35).

As the process of concentration and centralization of income and wealth moved full speed ahead during the Reagan Administration in the 1980s, the continuing class polarization has widened the gap between labor and capital still further during the 1990s and placed the workers into a desperate situation, facing indebtedness, economic uncertainty, and fear in securing the basic necessities of life, such as food, housing, and health care, for themselves and for their families.

EMERGING CLASS STRUGGLES
IN THE UNITED STATES

The persistent crisis of the U.S. economy in the 1970s and 1980s has had a contradictory effect on state and class politics in the United States during the 1990s. On the one hand, there has been a sharp turn to the right, as manifested in the rise of the New Right and right-wing religious fundamentalism, an all out assault on labor, reversals of civil rights gains, attacks on women's rights, a repressive immigration policy, renewed militarization, an increase in FBI domestic surveillance, and covert Central Intelligence Agency operations to accompany an interventionist policy in Central America, the Middle East, and elsewhere (Parenti 1995). On the other hand, there has been a rise in the militancy of workers and other progressive forces in society in response to this assault.

As the crisis of the capitalist economy has brought the advanced capitalist state to the center stage of economic life and revealed its direct ties to the monopolies,[7] thus exacerbating the state's legitimation crisis, the struggles of the working class and the masses in general are becoming increasingly political and are directed not merely against capital, but against the state itself. This transformation of the workers' struggle from the economic to the political sphere will set the stage for protracted working-class struggles in the years ahead.

While capital's answer to the growing ills of the U.S. economy has been further repression of the working-class and people's movements by the capitalist state, working people across the country have taken the initiative to struggle against the system through strikes, protests, demonstrations, and other forms of defiance. These actions are clear examples of an increasing class consciousness within the U.S. working class; they are taking place in the context of an intensifying worldwide capitalist crisis and in the midst of a much more politicized international labor movement, from the Philippines and South Korea to Central and South America, western Europe, and elsewhere around the world (Howard 1995; Bina and Davis 2002).

The globalization of U.S. capital is bound to accelerate the politicization of the U.S. working class and lead to the building of a solid foundation for international solidarity of workers on a world scale, directed against transnational capital and the advanced capitalist state in labor's long-term struggle for state power.

NOTES

1. I would argue that, while the massive 508-point drop in the stock market on "Black Monday" in October 1987 was a reflection of the long-term structural defects

of the financial system and the economy in general, it has actually proven itself to be an early indicator of a general decline of the stock market (especially NASDAQ stocks) in the early years of the twenty-first century. In fact, the drop in value of NAS-DAQ stocks, led by the high-tech computer industry, has been devastating with an overall decline from the 5,000 level in early 2000 to the 1,300 level in early 2003. Likewise, though not as dramatic, the Dow Jones industrial average declined from the 11,000 level in early 2000 to the 7,000 level in early 2003.

2. In 1999, there were 9,599 mergers totaling $3.4 trillion, up from $206 billion in 1990 (U.S. Bureau of the Census 2000, 551).

3. It is now estimated that more than 50 percent of all imports entering the United States are goods produced by overseas subsidiaries of U.S. transnational corporations. In addition, a substantial part of the remainder are produced through subcontracting arrangements between U.S. transnational and local firms—goods produced in accordance with U.S. corporate specifications for sale at major U.S. retail outlets.

4. In contrast with this, the inflation rate in the 1960s (a period of enormous war profits from the continuing war in Vietnam) was extremely low—about 1 percent per year in the early 1960s and 3 percent per year in the late 1960s (U.S. Bureau of the Census 1987, 455).

5. Except for 1981, when the rate was 10.3 percent, annual increases in the inflation rate have averaged between 3 and 5 percent during the rest of the 1980s, and between 2 and 3 percent during much of the 1990s (U.S. Council of Economic Advisers 2001, 343).

6. It should also be noted that actual gross profits of corporations are often understated, through such practices as intrafirm trade and transfer pricing, in order to reduce tax liabilities across national boundaries. Thus, the ratio of gross profits to net profits for many of the largest U.S. transnational corporations may well be higher than can be calculated from the reported Internal Revenue Service statistics.

7. For a detailed discussion on the relationship of the state to capital and the mechanisms of direct and indirect domination of the state by capital, see Szymanski (1978, 163–273); see also Parenti (2002a) and Domhoff (1998).

Chapter Eight

The Globalization of Capital and the Capitalist State in the Third World

This chapter examines the nature and role of the capitalist state in the Third World in the context of the globalization of capital and capitalist development over the course of the twentieth century. In this context, I examine the origins and development of the state in different regions of the Third World and outline the historical roots of the contemporary capitalist states that dominate the great majority of countries in Latin America, Asia, and Africa.

In general, the class forces that have been active in control of the capitalist state in the Third World are the local bourgeoisie (consisting of national and comprador segments), the large landowners, and the transnational corporations and their imperial states. The bureaucratic political-military apparatuses of the peripheral capitalist states have always operated within the framework of control of the state by one or a combination of these class forces whose class interests are implemented by the state's authoritarian, repressive bureaucratic machine.

In societies dominated by big landowners and the comprador bourgeoisie dependent on imperialism, the state has taken on a neocolonial character; and its survival is based on its role as an appendage of the transnational monopolies and the imperial state. In these societies, the state has become increasingly repressive and authoritarian in order to crush any popular opposition to its role in promoting the interests of local and transnational capitalist interests. As the states in these settings have found it necessary to legitimize their increasingly unpopular rule to maintain law and order, to protect private property, and to prevent a revolution against the prevailing social order, they have attempted to convey a "technocratic" image with focus on capital accumulation and economic growth, combined with severe repression of labor and other popular sectors of society.

Characterized by some as "corporatist" and by others as "bureaucratic authoritarian," or even "neofascist," the neocolonial capitalist states have played a key role in the globalization of capital and its predominance in much of the Third World, promoting further penetration of their economies and societies by the transnational monopolies.[1] This process of integration of neocolonial states into the global economy, seeking the protection of the imperial state, has been to a large degree a reaction to a perceived threat to the survival of capitalism in the Third World—one that is becoming a grave concern for both imperialism and the local repressive capitalist states.

The development of capitalism and the capitalist state in the Third World has been uneven chiefly because of variations in local precapitalist modes of production but also as a result of the nature and duration of contact with outside capitalist formations. This process took place during the period of Western colonialism and imperialism on a global scale, which began in the sixteenth century. The changes effected by this interaction yielded different results in different regions and led to alternative paths of development in Latin America, Asia, and Africa. This, in turn, gave way to the emergence and development of variants of the capitalist state throughout the Third World.

GLOBAL CAPITAL AND THE STATE
IN LATIN AMERICA

Prior to European expansion to the New World in the sixteenth century, the dominant mode of production in the Americas was tributary (i.e., the Asiatic mode of production) in some areas and tribal (i.e., the primitive communal mode) in others. In Mexico, much of Central America, and vast areas of South America, the Asiatic mode predominated in the Inca, Aztec, and Mayan empires. The central state, which had ultimate property rights, was the dominant force in society; peasants lived in villages and were obliged to pay tribute to the state. In North America, parts of the Caribbean, and some areas of South America, the primitive communal mode of production predominated among indigenous tribes. These societies were classless and stateless; they relied on hunting, fishing, gathering, and some early forms of horticulture for their subsistence. Lack of a substantial surplus and relative distance from aggressive empires prevented them from evolving toward a tributary mode through the emergence or imposition of a parasitic state. These formations remained intact until the arrival of the European colonizers in the early sixteenth century, which brought about major transformations in tributary and tribal societies throughout the New World. The colonization of the Americas began at a time when Spain was in transition from feudalism to capitalism, with feudalism still dominant. Spanish expansion into the New World was characterized by plunder of the newly acquired colonies. Gradually, the imposition of lord-serf relations (through the introduction of the haciendas) led to the establishment of feudal relations of production in the territories controlled by Spain.

The colonial expansion of Europe to the New World also facilitated the development of capitalism in Europe and led to its later spread to the colonies. With the development of European capitalism in the eighteenth century, trade with the colonies increasingly took on a capitalist character. As a result, alongside the feudal landowning class in the colonies, a class of merchants developed that was tied to the world market controlled by European commercial interests. In time, some of these merchants expanded into industrial pursuits and set the basis for capitalist development. Small-scale manufacturing, based on wage-labor, began to take root in the colonies and provided an outlet for capital accumulation among a section of the propertied elite. Nevertheless, the feudal landowning class and its political ally, the commercial bourgeoisie, remained the dominant economic and political forces in the colonies even after independence.

In the early nineteenth century, while the main sources of wealth in Latin America were controlled by the local propertied classes, political power was monopolized by the Spanish Crown. This division of economic and political control of Latin colonies served as the principal source of conflict between the Creole[2] bourgeoisie and Spain.

The independence movement of the nineteenth century was an attempt to obtain political autonomy from Spain. From 1830 to 1880, most of the newly formed nations of Latin America underwent a series of brutal civil wars. Federalists, provincialists, nationalists (both economic and political), and manufacturers stood on one side; unitarists, Latin American free traders, exporters and importers, landowners, and British and French imperialism were on the other side (Frank 1967). These groups opposed one another in a seemingly perpetual battle that lasted for decades. In the end, the latter group emerged victorious. The victory, first a political and military one and subsequently an economic one, subjugated the industrial and internally oriented national bourgeoisie. It was the beginning of an intimate relationship between British imperialism and the externally oriented Latin American commercial bourgeoisie, which implemented policies that would promote its interests. The end result of these policies was the concentration of income in the hands of compradors tied to the world economy that was dominated by British imperialism.

During the period of British imperialism, Latin American economies were thoroughly penetrated by British capital. Such penetration manifested itself in the direct control of raw materials by British interests. The investment of foreign capital in the Latin economy consequently integrated the Latin bourgeoisie into the global system in such a way that most Latin American countries became semicolonies of the expanding British Empire.

The outbreak of major global crises during the first half of the twentieth century brought about important changes in the external relations and internal structures of the majority of Latin American countries. The disruption of world trade during World War I was to be intensified by the Great Depression of the 1930s and by World War II. The decline in foreign trade and foreign capital substantially weakened Latin America's economic ties with Britain. These changes in the structure of the world economy created economic conditions and allowed political changes in Latin America that were to begin the region's strongest nationalist policy and largest independent industrialization drive since the 1830s (Furtado 1970). The drive subsequently opened for the Latin American industrial bourgeoisie the period of import-substituting industrialization directed toward the diversification of the production structure in manufactures. International crises thus freed Latin America from outright subordination to imperial centers and accelerated its growth toward independent capitalist development. During this period, the state came under the control of the national bourgeoisie, whose interests dictated the development of a strong capitalist state.

The ascendancy of the United States in the Western Hemisphere after World War II, resulting from Britain's declining economic power and near defeat during the war, effected the interimperialist transfer of control over Latin America from Britain to the United States (Petras and Morley 1997). U.S. economic expansion to Latin America accelerated during the 1950s, as the United States began to rely increasingly on strategic raw materials from abroad. The need for metals and minerals brought about a rapid expansion of U.S. investment in Latin America in subsequent decades. While extractive industries (e.g., petroleum and mining) continued throughout the 1950s and 1960s to constitute an important part of U.S. investment in Latin America, by the mid-1960s the pattern of U.S. economic penetration in the hemisphere had taken on new forms. From this point onward, U.S.-based transnational corporations began to penetrate the national industries of Latin America and to control the manufacturing sector developed by the local industrial bourgeoisie. As a result, the independent industrialization process initiated by the national bourgeoisie in the more advanced countries of the region in the 1930s was gradually transformed, and their economies became dependent on the world economy dominated by the U.S. transnationals (Cardoso and Faletto 1979; Cockcroft 1996). Moving them in the direction of export-oriented satellites as they fulfilled their role in the new international division of labor, the economic changes effected by this new relationship required the introduction of political changes as well. Repressive military rule was needed to stabilize the dependent social order (Boron 1995). The "democratic" capitalist state of an earlier period—in Brazil, Argentina, Chile, Peru, and else-where—gave way to the authoritarian and repressive neocolonial capitalist state, followed by a transition to civilian rule orchestrated by the military (Buxton and Phillips 1999).

With the rapid expansion of U.S. capital to Latin America in the postwar period, capitalist development in the region during this period brought about a transformation in the balance of class forces and transferred state power into the hands of comprador elements tied to the transnationals and the U.S. imperial state (Halebsky and Harris 1995). And in the post–Cold War unipolar world of globalization, this linkage to the current center of world imperialism has been further strengthened through renewed integration of the Latin economies into the structure of the "new world order" dominated by the United States (Roy 1999; Petras 2002). As a result, the state in much of Latin America has continued to more closely serve the interests of foreign capital and its internal neocolonial agents under conditions of imperialist control and domination that characterizes this most recent period of globalization.[3]

GLOBAL CAPITAL AND THE STATE IN ASIA

Vast areas of Asia were colonized by Western powers until the middle of the twentieth century. British and European capital mercilessly plundered these regions at the height of their empires. Through their presence in the area, they effected major changes in the social and economic structures of the societies of Asia that they came to dominate and thus greatly affected the character of the state that they came to control and rule. Feudal relations of production were introduced in Spain's Asian colony, the Philippines; the slave mode was introduced and despotic rule was reinforced in Java and other parts of colonial Indonesia by the Dutch; and capitalism made headway in British India and British-controlled parts of Southeast Asia.

In India, antagonism between British and local industrial capital led to the national bourgeois alliance with the peasantry to throw off the British yoke through the independence movement (Chandra 1975). Much as in North America, but unlike the situation in Latin America, the national bourgeois forces were able to consolidate power and capture the leadership of the movement in a victory over the British. By the late 1940s, they installed a state committed to the development of local capitalism in India following independence. Given the relatively weak position of the national bourgeoisie, the victorious petit bourgeois nationalist forces were able to utilize the powers of the state and establish a state-capitalist regime to assist the accumulation of capital by the Indian bourgeoisie (Levkovsky 1966).

In the period following independence in 1947, the state played an important role in accelerating the development of capitalism. Industrial production grew at a rapid rate, as did total productive capital in large-scale industries. The most significant growth took place in capital goods industries (Sen 1982). This growth in the first two decades following independence led to a steady increase in the share of industry in the gross domestic product (GDP). The development of private industry in the postindependence period, together with the expansion of state enterprises since the 1950s, accelerated the development of capitalism and the capitalist state, thus securing the domination of capitalism and capitalist relations of production (Desai 1984). This process in turn gave rise to a large working class. The number of wage earners in India doubled between 1951 and 1971—reaching more than twenty-three million—and grew further during the 1970s, 1980s, and 1990s, to a total of twenty-eight million in 1996 (International Labor Office 1998, 311).

With the growth of the working class, the conflict between labor and capital intensified. The capitalist assault on workers' wages and democratic rights met stiff resistance from organized labor and the trade union movement and led to the radicalization of large segments of the working class, whose demands became increasingly political. Threatened with these developments and fearful of a general social explosion based on a revolutionary alliance of workers and peasants, the bourgeois state became more repressive; it also opened its doors to transnational monopolies, thus seeking refuge in imperialism (Sau 1992).

Over the years, the United States gradually replaced British control over India and emerged as a powerful force with the promotion of the Green Revolution in the 1960s. Thus, while the British share in total foreign investment in the private sector was roughly 80 percent in 1948, it fell to 48 percent by the mid-1960s; in contrast, the U.S. share in total private foreign investment increased from 4 percent in 1949 to 25 percent by the mid-1960s (Chattopadhyay 1992). This trend continued during the 1970s and 1980s and accelerated during the 1990s. Today, at the turn of the twenty-first century U.S. transnationals, along with the Indian bourgeoisie, control the "commanding heights" of the Indian economy. And the capitalist state in India has played a central role in facilitating the development of capitalism within the framework of the global capitalist economy dominated by U.S. imperialism (Desai 1984).

A move from a state-capitalist to a neocolonial comprador-capitalist path tied to foreign capital is the typical outcome of a state-capitalist formation developing within the parameters of the global capitalist system. India, like many other state-capitalist regimes in the Third World, has not been able to escape from this general rule of capitalist development in the age of imperialism. Its development within the context of the global economy has resulted in massive economic dislocations and crises over the past two decades and has led to further consolidation of the reactionary forces' grip over the state in more fully integrating India into the global capitalist system. This, in turn, has galvanized popular opposition forces in their struggle against the capitalist state and has given new impetus to their efforts to transform Indian society (Kotovsky 1992; Tharamangalam 1992).

Elsewhere in East and Southeast Asia, a number of states emerged as appendages of the global capitalist system following World War II. Evolving as neocolonies of the expanding U.S. empire in the postwar period, these states came to serve the economic and strategic interests of U.S. monopolies and the state in providing cheap labor, raw materials, new markets, new investment outlets, and a military foothold throughout the area to protect transnational interests and encircle and contain socialist states in the region. South Korea, Taiwan, the Philippines, Indonesia, Thailand, Malaysia, Hong Kong, Singapore, Cambodia, and South Vietnam (until 1975) served one or more of these functions and provided the material base for U.S. transnational expansion in the area after the fall of Japan at the end of the war. By the early 1950s, South Korea, Taiwan, and the Philippines, together with defeated Japan, came under the U.S. military umbrella in the Pacific Basin and provided a foundation for the expansion of U.S. transnational corporations in these countries (Green 1971; Szymanski 1981; Parenti 1989, 1995).

A similar development in South Vietnam, Cambodia, Laos, and Thailand in the aftermath of the British and French defeat in the region brought the United States into the conflict there during the late 1950s and early 1960s. The U.S. military escalation in Southeast Asia expanded the conflict into one of the biggest wars in the region's recent history—one that lasted over three decades. However, by the mid-1970s U.S. efforts at domination over the region collapsed, as the Indo-Chinese people drove the U.S. forces out of their territories. With Vietnam, Cambodia, and Laos out of the U.S. grip, Thailand, Indonesia, South Korea, and especially the Philippines took on the role of regional policemen to protect U.S. interests in East and Southeast Asia and provide security for regional operations of the U.S. transnationals. Thus, while U.S. military presence in or economic aid to these countries turned them into de facto neocolonial capitalist states, their subsequent economic integration into the global capitalist system transformed their social and economic structures to suit the needs of U.S. and other transnational monopolies (Clark and Kim 1995). They advanced along the capitalist path, with high growth rates and profits for foreign and local capitalists on the one hand, and the exploitation of workers and peasants on the other (Wynn 1982; Hamilton 1983; Lindsey 1985).

With the expansion of U.S. capital in East and Southeast Asia in the 1960s and 1970s, these regions became more fully integrated into the global economy. Through such investments and other economic arrangements, these states began to fulfill their special role in the international division of labor controlled by the U.S. transnational monopolies (Hamilton 1983, 1986; Patnaik 1999; Kim 2000).[4] This prompted increased foreign investment and subcontracting with local firms for the production of commodities for export destined for markets in the advanced capitalist countries. As a result, the globalization of capital has further facilitated the rapid expansion of capitalism and the capitalist state in these countries with high levels of corruption, leading to the development of what some have called "crony capitalism" (Kang 2002).

The development of capitalism and the capitalist state through this process exacerbated larger social, economic, and political problems confronting these countries, including employment at very low wages, control over the technology transferred to the recipient country, and draining of profits made from the sale of exported goods—problems that have impeded the full-scale development of capitalism in this region (Patnaik 1999). Additionally, this process has led to:

1. The destruction of an integrated national economy and the installation of enclave export zones controlled by transnational firms
2. The bankruptcy of small- and medium-size businesses and the monopolization of the local economy by foreign capital
3. Income inequalities based on an internal market dependent on no more than 5 percent of the population
4. Low wages leading to a decline in the standard of living of the majority of the population with its attendant consequences on diet, housing, health care, education, and other needs
5. Rising unemployment, poverty, malnutrition, and related ills
6. Social and political repression through the installation of brutal (often military) dictatorships that violate basic human rights (Bello and Rosenfeld 1990).

These effects of transnational capitalism in states under the grip of foreign capital are the outcome of a system of relations imposed on working people by imperialism, which is based on the exploitation of the working class and the peasantry (Parenti 1995). The social significance of global capitalist expansion in these regions lies in the transformation of local relations of production in a capitalist direction and the consolidation of a capitalist state that is subservient to imperialism, with all its inherent class contradictions.

The increase in number of workers in the manufacturing sector and, more broadly, in all major branches of industry, accompanied by below-subsistence wages and antilabor legislation enacted by repressive capitalist states, have led to the intensification of the class struggle in these countries, with some of them (e.g., South Korea, the Philippines, and Indonesia) reaching a near-revolutionary stage, as the masses challenge the rule of the neocolonial capitalist state (Hart-Landsberg 1993; McNally 1998).

GLOBAL CAPITAL AND THE STATE IN AFRICA

Prior to European intervention, Africa had a diverse social structure based on various modes of production in different regions of the continent. The primitive communal mode was dominant in some areas, and the Asiatic and feudal modes were paramount in others. Although slavery was practiced in various parts of the continent before the European-initiated slave trade, it never became a dominant mode of production in precolonial Africa. Primitive communal relations of production were prevalent in central and parts of southern Africa, while the Asiatic mode dominated much of North Africa until the end of the nineteenth century. Feudalism in various forms was practiced in parts of East and West Africa.[5]

Despite the prevalence of these diverse modes in various parts of the continent, precolonial Africa consisted in large part of self-sufficient village communities engaged in subsistence agriculture. Where feudalism or a despotic state existed, villagers provided a surplus to the ruling classes in the form of a tribute or a part of their produce. With the widespread introduction of the slave trade by European imperialism, greater stratification was induced in the continent, and many newly created tribal chiefs were corrupted by European conquerors and turned into tyrants serving the interests of Western imperialism. The artificial creation of "district chiefs" in the French colonies and of "headmen" in the English colonies was done for this purpose (Harris 1975). After the sixteenth century, when the world economy facilitated the spread of the slave trade in Africa, slaves become Africa's major export; they were bought and sold to masters in various parts of the world, especially in the Americas (Davidson 1961).

The slave trade inhibited indigenous capital accumulation and thus the development of local capitalism, as it deprived Africa of able-bodied workers, undermined local artisan production because of the cheap European goods received for the slaves, and reinforced slavery as a mode of production. The economic development that did take place during this period was highly dependent on the European colonial economy tied to the slave trade (Rodney 1972). With the end of the slave trade in the first half of the nineteenth century, African economies shifted to commercial export crops. Commodities such as cocoa, peanuts, palm oil, coffee, and rubber became the principle exports. As a result, the previously dominant ruling classes, whose wealth and power were based on the slave trade, transformed themselves into planters who imposed semifeudal production relations on their former slaves, who now labored on vast plantations in serflike conditions.

The wealth and power of the local ruling class declined during the course of the nineteenth century as European colonialism gained a more direct foothold in the continent and became involved in production and trade throughout the region (Harris 1975). By the end of the nineteenth century, the European powers had moved in with full force against local states and chiefdoms and set up colonial regimes. Labor migration became the main mechanism to secure a labor force in the mining sector, as well as in commercial crop production. Africans engaged in subsistence production on communal lands were manipulated into providing labor to the Europeans, who introduced taxes payable in money. In this way, they were able to force Africans to work in European-owned enterprises to secure the means to pay their taxes (Nabudere 1981). At the same time, labor services (*corvée*) were introduced, although they could often be avoided in exchange for a cash payment. To avoid corvée, one had to prove gainful employment. Either way, the European colonialists were the only ones to gain from these practices.

In time, the notion of private property was introduced, which undermined traditional subsistence agriculture and led to increased demands for commercial goods. This provided sufficient incentive to get Africans to sell their labor power for a wage. Over the years, the African economies became increasingly commercial, wage-labor became more prevalent, raw material exports grew, and the demand for European industrial imports increased. As a result, Africa evolved along the capitalist path tied to the European-dominated world economy, which at the end of the nineteenth and beginning of the twentieth centuries had transformed Africa by introducing capitalist relations of production into the continent through colonial rule (Szymanski 1981).

The different forms of exploitation and the different class structures, hence the varied forms of the state, that developed during the colonial era in various colonized regions of Africa can thus be explained in terms of the different modes of production prevailing in Europe and in the colonies, as well as the interaction between the two at different points in history. In this sense, the precapitalist imperialism of Portugal in Angola, Mozambique, and other Portuguese colonies in Africa produced a legacy of feudalism, while the capitalist imperialism of a more developed industrial Britain in transition to monopoly capital at a later period produced a qualitatively different result in the British colonies throughout Africa, where capitalist relations of production began to take root (Berberoglu 1987b).

Until the middle of the twentieth century, when most African countries won their formal independence, the local economies were a direct appendage of the colonial center, which directed development in the colonies. The pattern was based on the logic of the capitalist mode of production that dominated the economies of the center states and evolved according to its needs of accumulation, resulting in uneven development between the imperial center and the colonies, and within the colonies. As a result, most African colonies specialized in one or a few raw materials for export and depended on the importation of finished manufactured goods from the imperial center, a condition that led to their underdevelopment (Rodney 1972; Nabudere 1981).

This classic colonial relationship prevailed in a number of African countries after the granting of formal independence and led to the restructuring of socioeconomic relations on a neocolonial basis—that is, the continuation of colonial relations through the intermediary of a local ruling class dependent on imperialism. This has been the case in various parts of the continent, from Kenya in the east, to Nigeria and the Ivory Coast in the west, to Zaire, Cameroon, Zimbabwe, and other countries in central and southern Africa (Leys 1975). As in the colonial period, the main characteristic of these neocolonial capitalist states is their heavy reliance on the export of raw materials to the advanced capitalist countries and the import of manufactured goods from them, which has become an impediment to industrialization and holds back the development of the industrial sector in these countries (Saul and Leys 1999).

Within this broader framework of the neocolonial structure, there has nevertheless occurred a parallel development of transnational corporate expansion into the manufacturing sector of some of these countries in order to utilize cheap labor in a variety of manufacturing and industrial undertakings. This has contributed to the growth of the industrial sector and effected changes in the sectorial distribution of the gross domestic product (GDP) in favor of industry. As a result, the share of industry relative to agriculture has increased over time. This is most evident in western and northern Africa, notably in Nigeria, Liberia, Ivory Coast, Tunisia, and Egypt.

Despite the fact that the pace of industrialization in these countries is considerably slower than in Latin America and East and Southeast Asia, the move in the direction of investments in industry has brought about a significant change in the economic and labor force structure of these countries and placed them on the road to further capitalist development within the bounds of the global economy. Thus, while neocolonial African states continue to remain primarily agricultural or raw material exporting countries, the relative growth of manufacturing and other industry vis-à-vis agriculture indicates an overall trend toward industrialization within a neocolonial capitalist framework tied to imperialism (Mahjoub 1990).

In other African countries, such as the Sudan, Uganda, and Zaire, semifeudal relations based on raw material production continue with little progress on the industrial front. This shows the dual nature of imperialist penetration in different regions and countries of the continent where traditional colonial relations are reinforced in some areas, while comprador-capitalist neocolonial relations are developed and strengthened in others.

Elsewhere in Africa, nationalist forces have taken the initiative to lead the newly independent states along a less dependent path. Utilizing the military and state bureaucracy as supportive institutions to carry out their development programs, the petit bourgeois leaders in these countries have opted for a state-capitalist path through the establishment of state-owned enterprises, public works projects, and so on. Gamal Abdel Nasser in Egypt, Houari Boumedienne in Algeria, and Kenneth D. Kaunda in Zambia could be cited as prime examples of petit bourgeois nationalist leaders in charge of postcolonial states developing along the state-capitalist path. Unlike neocolonial capitalist states, such as Zaire under Joseph Désiré Mobutu and Ethiopia under Haile Selassie, the national state-capitalist formations of Africa became the leading force on the continent in the first decades of the postcolonial period.

Historically, the presence of a racist apartheid regime in South Africa has been a great impediment to the development of revolutionary forces in the southern cone of Africa and has had a major impact on the scope and pace of development on the continent in a progressive direction. With the abolition of the apartheid regime in South Africa in the 1990s, however, the last vestiges of racist colonial and neocolonial oppression have been formally removed, so that an open political struggle could be waged by the masses to take control of their destiny and build a new state and society (Nash 1999).

GLOBAL CAPITAL, THE STATE, AND SOCIAL TRANSFORMATION IN THE THIRD WORLD

The historical development of capitalism and capitalist states in different regions of the Third World illustrate the varied nature and dynamics of societies that have evolved out of interaction between local, precapitalist modes of production and capitalism originating in Europe and other colonial and imperial centers of the global economy.

In some regions, such as Latin America and parts of Asia, Africa, and the Middle East, the Oriental despotic state was overrun by European colonialism. Feudal land-tenure practices were introduced, together with merchants' capital tied to the colonial center. Despite revolts against the European colonial empires, the introduction of feudal and commercial modes of production had a profound effect on the later development of capitalism and the capitalist state in these areas. Despite formal independence from the center states, they developed as appendages of them. This relationship continued despite shifts in power in the colonial centers, so that the transition from colonial status did not alter the underlying relationship between the ruling classes in the former colonies and the center states. Remnants of feudal landed and commercial moneyed interests lingered on in the context of an emerging local capitalist class in a changing global economy that accommodated all three segments. Within this framework of the colonial and neocolonial states in these regions, there resulted the development of two variants of the neocolonial capitalist state: the semifeudal/semicapitalist and the more developed comprador capitalist. While they have a similar political relationship with the imperialist centers, these two variants of the capitalist state are nevertheless ruled by classes that occupy different positions in the social and economic structure.

Prevailing in much of the less developed capitalist world, the comprador-capitalist states are the main variant of the capitalist state in the Third World today. The dominant mode of production in comprador-capitalist formations, such as Brazil, Mexico, Argentina, South Korea, Taiwan, the Philippines, Iran under the Shah, and Turkey, is capitalist, with precapitalist (i.e., feudal and/or transitional petty commodity) modes surviving in the countryside and sometimes exercising considerable influence within their domain. The expansion of foreign investment in manufacturing, agriculture, and raw materials in these countries since the early 1960s has accelerated the process of capitalist development so that previously precapitalist production relations have been transformed into capitalist ones. With the spread of capitalism and capitalist relations in these formations, state power has increasingly come under the influence and later control of the comprador capitalists,[6] as the traditional alliance of landlords and compradors has proven to be an obstacle to the further expansion of the economic interests of the local bourgeoisie collaborating with imperialism. The change in relations between imperialism and the local ruling classes came in the 1960s in many parts of the Third World: In Latin America, it coincided with and was reinforced by the so-called Alliance for Progress; in Asia, it came with the Green Revolution in India; in the Middle East, it was facilitated by the White Revolution in Iran and by the Menderes regime in Turkey; and in Africa, it came with the transition from colonial rule to independence.

In these and other comprador-capitalist formations, state power is no longer shared equally between landlords and compradors, but it is in the hands of comprador capitalists tied to imperialism. At the current stage of development of these neocolonial capitalist states, the comprador-imperialist alliance is directed against the precapitalist landowning class for the transformation of the countryside into capitalist agriculture. Mechanization and wage-labor, introduced and expanded by transnational agricultural monopolies, are part of the ongoing consolidation of these states into the global capitalist economy that is dominated and controlled by the bourgeoisie of the advanced capitalist formations, particularly the United States.

The transformation of the internal social structure of comprador-capitalist states has been most visible in formations receiving the greatest amount of foreign (primarily U.S.) manufacturing investments since the early 1960s. Largely as a result of these investments, there has occurred a high rate of growth in the manufacturing sector, signifying the new relationship between local comprador capitalists and imperialism as these countries have come to serve the special needs of the transnational monopolies, especially the need for cheap labor.

Nevertheless, the expansion of foreign capital into the local economy through the intermediary of the comprador bourgeoisie has increasingly become a threat to national and petit bourgeois sectors, giving rise to nationalist sentiments among them. More fundamentally, the unfolding process of dependent development, which has accelerated the spread of capitalist production relations in these formations, has given rise to the growth of an increasingly militant working class that is beginning to challenge the prevailing comprador-capitalist power structure.

Unlike the current neocolonial comprador-capitalist states, but similar to their earlier stage of development, state power in semifeudal/semicapitalist formations (e.g., Guatemala, El Salvador, Paraguay, Zaire, Bangladesh, Oman, and Saudi Arabia) is shared by comprador capitalists and precapitalist landowners tied to imperialism, although the landowners constitute the dominant force within the alliance. Clearly, landowners in these formations are not capitalists, but have a feudal, semifeudal, or despotic character, depending on the formation. The labor force in the countryside remains outside wage relations, as payment in kind and the accompanying lord-serf production relationship persist.

Although feudal or semifeudal relations continue in the villages, this does not mean that large landowners function in isolation from the capitalist mode of production and exchange. In fact, they are an integral part of the larger semifeudal/semicapitalist formation and are actively engaged in a variety of capitalist activities, including import-export trade, banking, shipping and transport, marketing, raw material extraction, and even manufacturing. Indeed, the expanded capitalist economic activities of an otherwise precapitalist landowning class explains well the convergence of the interests of landlords and compradors as the dominant ruling classes in these formations, hence the sharing of state power between them. While a tendency exists for commercially involved landowners to become part of a single ruling comprador-capitalist class, a countertendency also exists. Comprador elements allied with transnational monopolies expand to the countryside to transform the landowning class along capitalist lines, followed by an erosion of the power of landlords in the state apparatus. This signals the transition of the semifeudal/semicapitalist state to its later comprador-capitalist form.

Given the low level of development of the productive forces and the importance of agriculture and raw materials production in these states, foreign penetration and domination of the local economy is carried out through the intermediary of the landowning class: the dominant class within the landlord-comprador state. Thus, while the domination of compradors in neocolonial comprador-capitalist states has opened the way for capitalist industrialization from the outside, the domination of the landlord class in semifeudal/semicapitalist states, together with the latter's traditional role as suppliers of raw materials and/or agricultural products, has stifled capitalist expansion in these formations. As a result, these states have been locked into a position of specialization in line with the raw material needs of the transnational monopolies.

The variation in the economies of these different sets of neocolonial capitalist states tells us something about the effects generated by the relations between imperialism and dominant class forces. These relations reinforce a development pattern that either perpetuates *or* restructures socioeconomic forms, thus affecting the class structure and the form of the state in different ways. It is in terms of the significance of this latter effect that a differentiation of the nature of the capitalist states in the Third World becomes so important.

NOTES

1. On corporatist interpretations of the peripheral state, see Stepan (1978). On bureaucratic authoritarianism, see O'Donnell (1973, 1979). On the neofascist character of dependent states ruled by military dictatorships, see Petras (1981). For a discussion on the nature of the bureaucratic authoritarian and other forms of the dependent state, see Berberoglu (1987a, 1987b); see also Carnoy (1984, chapter 7).

2. This term refers to native-born Latin Americans of Spanish descent.

3. The notable exceptions to this are the recent administrations in Venezuela and Brazil, where populist president Hugo Chavez in Venezuela since 1998 and the popular labor leader Luiz Inacio Lula da Silva, commonly known as "Lula," who won a landslide victory in the Brazilian presidential elections of October 2002, have followed an independent policy that is not subservient to imperialist interests.

4. Thus, while large investments were made in the Indonesian oil industry, countries such as South Korea, Taiwan, Hong Kong, Singapore, and the Philippines came to serve as cheap labor reserves, and Hong Kong and Singapore took on additional roles as important financial and trade centers for the Western monopolies. Moreover, South Korea, the Philippines, and Thailand took up the further strategic role of providing a military shield in the area for the expansion of the newly established export-oriented economies (Hamilton 1983; Bello and Rosenfeld 1990).

5. Feudalism practiced in these regions, especially in the East, however, was based mainly on control of cattle, rather than of land, as in Europe.

6. Comprador capitalists are those capitalists mainly concentrated in import-export commerce and are directly tied to the imperial centers due to their trade relations with the imperialist countries.

Chapter Nine

Globalization, Class Struggle, and Social Transformation

We live in the age of global capitalism. During the twentieth century, capital became thoroughly global. Today, we live in a world dominated by the transnational monopolies that control every aspect of life, including first and foremost politics and the state. They are the appropriators of surplus value through the exploitation of the great majority of the world's population—that is, through the exploitation of labor. Capital in this way has become over the past two centuries the primary driving force in social, economic, and political affairs. In the process of this expansion and domination, however, capitalism has undergone to experience its inherent contradictions in a most decisive way: While the expansion of capital worldwide has generated immense profits for the transnationals, it has at the same time plunged the domestic economies of the imperialist states into a permanent crisis—one that facilitates the intensification of the class struggle against transnational capital on a global level.

In this final chapter, I examine the contradictions and crisis of global capitalism, the relationship between globalization and imperialism, the developing class struggle, and the prospects for social change and transformation of global capitalism. I examine these within the context of the globalization of capital in the twentieth century and map out the political implications of this process for the future course of development of capitalism on a world scale from the angle of the working class and the class struggle between labor and capital in the age of global capitalism.

THE CRISIS OF GLOBAL CAPITALISM

The development of capitalism over the past hundred years formed and transformed capitalist society in a crucial way, one characterized by periodic crises effected by the business cycle that now unfolds on a global level (Steven 1994). The latest crisis of global capitalism is the result of the consolidation of monopoly power through the globalization of capital effected by the transnational monopolies and manifests itself in a number of ways:

1. The problems arising from the contradiction between the expanded forces of production and existing exploitative class relations
2. The problem of overproduction, resulting from the imbalance created between wages and prices of commodities, leading to periodic recessions and depressions
3. Increasing unemployment resulting from continued application of technology in production (i.e., automation)
4. The restructuring of the international division of labor through the export of capital and transfer of production to cheap labor areas abroad, resulting in industrial decline and decay, hence greater unemployment in the center states
5. Intensification of the exploitation of labor through expanded production and reproduction of surplus value and profits by further accumulation of capital and the reproduction of capitalist relations of production on a world scale
6. Increased polarization of wealth and income at the national and global levels between the capitalist and working classes and growth in numbers of the poor and marginalized segments of the population throughout the world

These and other related contradictions of global capitalism define the parameters of modern, capitalist imperialism and provide us the framework of discussion on the nature and dynamics of imperialism and globalization in the world today.

Given the logic of global capital accumulation in late capitalist society, it is no accident that the decline of the domestic economy of advanced capitalist countries over the past two decades corresponds to the accelerated export of capital abroad in search of cheap labor, access to raw materials, new markets, and higher rates of profit. The resulting deindustrialization of the domestic economy has had a serious impact on workers and other affected segments of the laboring population and has brought about a major dislocation of the national economy (Phillips 1998).[1] This has necessitated increased state intervention on behalf of the monopolies and has heightened the contradictions that led to the crisis of advanced capitalist society.

The widening gap between the accumulated wealth of the capitalist class and the declining incomes of workers (within a deteriorating national economy and the state's budgetary crisis) has led to the ensuing political crisis within the state apparatus and has sharpened the class struggle in a new political direction. As the crisis of the capitalist economy has brought the advanced capitalist state to the center stage of economic life and revealed its direct ties to the monopolies, thus exacerbating the state's legitimation crisis, the struggles of the working class and the masses in general are becoming directed not merely against capital, but against the state itself (Beams 1998). This transformation of the workers' struggle from the economic to the political sphere will set the stage for protracted struggles in the period ahead—struggles that will take place in the context of an intensifying worldwide capitalist crisis and in the midst of a much more politicized international labor movement. The globalization of capital is thus bound to accelerate the politicization of the working class and lead to the building of a solid foundation for international solidarity of workers on a world scale that is directed against imperialism and the advanced capitalist state (Howard 1995; Bina and Davis 2002).

IMPERIALISM AND GLOBALIZATION

Imperialism is the highest stage of capitalism operating on a world scale, and globalization is the highest stage of imperialism that has penetrated every corner of the world. Both are an outgrowth of twentieth-century monopoly capitalism—an inevitable consequence, or manifestation, of monopoly capital that now dominates the world capitalist political economy (Halliday 2001). Thus, the current wave of globalization is an extension of this process that operates at a more advanced and accelerated level.

Today, in the early twenty-first century, the dominant institution that has facilitated global capitalist expansion on behalf of the current center of world imperialism since the post–World War II period—the United States—is the *transnational corporation* (Nabudere 1977; Barnet and Cavenagh 1994). As other capitalist rivals from Europe and the Pacific Basin have recently begun to emerge on the world scene as serious contenders for global economic power, they too have developed and unleashed their own transnational corporate and financial institutions to carve out greater profits, accumulate greater wealth, and thereby dominate the global economy. The transnational corporations and banks, based in the leading centers of world capitalism, have thus become the chief instruments of global capitalist expansion and capital accumulation (Waters 1995; Mittelman and Othman 2002). It is, therefore, in the export of capital and its expanded reproduction abroad to accumulate greater wealth for the capitalist classes of the advanced capitalist countries that one can find the motive force of imperialism in the world today.

The relationship between the owners of the transnational corporations—the monopoly capitalist class—and the imperialist state and the role and functions of this state, including the use of military force to advance the interests of the monopoly capitalist class, thus reveals the class nature of the imperialist state and the class logic of imperialism and globalization in the world today (Warren 1980; Szymanski 1981; Berberoglu 1987b, 1992b, 2001). But this logic is more pervasive and is based on a more fundamental class relation between labor and capital that now operates on a global level, that is, a relation based on exploitation. Thus, in the age of globalization, that is, in the epoch of capitalist imperialism, social classes and class struggles are a product of the logic of the global capitalist system based on the exploitation of labor worldwide (Gerstein 1977; Petras 1978; Berberoglu 1994).

Capitalist expansion on a world scale at this stage of the globalization of capital and capitalist production has brought with it the globalization of the production process and the exploitation of wage-labor on a world scale. With the intensified exploitation of the working class at super-low wages in repressive neocolonial societies throughout the Third World, the transnational corporations of the leading capitalist powers have come to amass great fortunes that they have used to build up a global empire through the powers of the imperial state, which has not hesitated to use its military power to protect and advance the interests of capital in every corner of the globe. It is in this context that we see the coalescence of the interests of the global economy and empire as manifested in control of cheap labor, new markets, and vital sources of raw materials, such as oil, and the intervention of the state to protect these when their continued supply to the imperial center are threatened. What better example of this can one think of than what is now taking place in the Middle East!

V. I. Lenin, in his book *Imperialism: The Highest Stage of Capitalism* ([1917] 1975), pointed out that capitalism in its highest and most mature monopoly stage has spread to every corner of the world and thus has planted the seeds of its own contradictions everywhere. The beginning point of Lenin's analysis of imperialism is his conception of the dynamics of modern capitalism: the concentration and centralization of production. "The enormous growth of industry and the remarkably rapid concentration of production in ever-larger enterprises," he wrote, "are one of the most characteristic features of capitalism" (642). Moreover, "at a certain stage of its development," he added, "concentration itself, as it were, leads straight to monopoly. . . . Today, monopoly has become a fact . . . and that the rise of monopolies, as a result of the concentration of production, is a general and fundamental law of the present stage of development of capitalism" (643, 645).

The underlying argument in Lenin's analysis of imperialism as the highest stage of capitalism is that imperialism is the necessary outcome of the development of capitalism:

> Imperialism emerged as the development and direct continuation of the fundamental characteristics of capitalism in general. But capitalism only became capitalist imperialism at a definite and very high stage of its development. . . . Economically, the main thing in this process is the displacement of capitalist free competition by capitalist monopoly. . . . Monopoly is the transition from capitalism to a higher system. If it were necessary to give the briefest possible definition of imperialism we should have to say that imperialism is the monopoly stage of capitalism. ([1917] 1975, 699–700)

Thus, in summarizing the fundamental features of imperialism, that is, monopoly capitalism operating on a world scale, Lenin concluded, "Imperialism is capitalism in that stage of development in which the dominance of monopolies and finance capital is established; in which the export of capital has acquired pronounced importance; in which the division of the world among the international trusts has begun; in which the division of all territories of the globe among the biggest capitalist powers has been completed" (700).

Lenin's emphasis on the importance of the export of capital is crucial from the angle of its implications concerning the transformation of relations of production abroad. With the export of capital as the primary source of the globalization of capital and capitalist class relations on a world scale, capitalism effected transformations in the class structure of societies with which it came into contact. As a result, the class contradictions of the capitalist mode of production became the outcome of the dominant form of exploitation of labor through the instrumentality of imperialist expansion throughout the world. It is in this context of the developing worldwide contradictions of advanced, monopoly capitalism that Lenin pointed out, "[I]mperialism is the eve of the social revolution of the proletariat . . . on a worldwide scale" ([1917] 1975, 640).

IMPERIALISM, GLOBALIZATION, AND CLASS STRUGGLE

Imperialist expansion has had varied effects in the international and domestic economic spheres. At the global level, it has meant first and foremost the ever-growing exploitation of workers through the use of cheap labor. In addition, it has caused a depletion of resources that could be used for national development, environmental pollution and other health hazards, a growing national debt tying many countries to the World Bank, the International Monetary Fund, and other imperialist financial institutions, and a growing militarization of society through the institution of brutal military and civilian dictatorships that violate basic human rights. The domination and control of Third World countries for transnational profits through the instrumentality of the imperialist state has at the same time created a culture and psychology of dependence on the center that has become part of life under globalization (Amaladoss 1999; Sklair 2002).

Domestically, the globalization of capital and imperialist expansion has had immense dislocations in the national economies of imperialist states. Expansion of manufacturing industry abroad has meant a decline in local industry, as plant closings in the United States and other advanced capitalist countries has worsened the unemployment situation. The massive expansion of capital abroad has resulted in hundreds of factory shutdowns with millions of workers losing their jobs, hence the surge in unemployment in the United States and other imperialist states (Wagner 2000). This has led to a decline in wages of workers in the advanced capitalist centers, as low wages abroad have played a competitive role in keeping wages down in the imperialist heartlands. The drop in incomes among a growing section of the working class has thus lowered the standard of living in general and led to a further polarization between labor and capital (Berberoglu 1992a, 2002).

The dialectics of global capitalist expansion, which has caused so much exploitation, oppression, and misery for the peoples of the world both in the Third World and in the imperialist countries themselves has, in turn, created the conditions for its own destruction. Economically, it has afflicted the system with recessions, depressions, and an associated realization crisis; politically, it has set into motion an imperial interventionist state that through its presence in every corner of the world has incurred an enormous military expenditure to maintain an empire, while gaining the resentment of millions of people across the globe who are engaged in active struggle against it.[2]

The imperial capitalist state, acting as the repressive arm of global capital and extending its rule across vast territories, has dwarfed the militaristic adventures of past empires many times over. The global capitalist state, through its political and military supremacy, has come to exert its control over many countries and facilitate the exploitation of labor on a world scale. As a result, it has reinforced the domination of capital over labor and its rule on behalf of capital. This, in turn, has greatly politicized the struggle between labor and capital and called for the recognition of the importance of political organization that many find it necessary to effect change in order to transform the capitalist-imperialist system.

Understanding the necessity of organizing labor and the importance of political leadership in this struggle, radical labor organizations have in fact taken steps emphasizing the necessity for the working class to mobilize its ranks and take united action to wage battle against capitalist imperialism globally (Waterman 1998; Munck and Waterman 1999; Siebert 2000; Nissen 2002). In this sense, labor internationalism (or the political alliance of workers across national boundaries in their struggle against global capitalism) is increasingly being seen as a political weapon that would serve as a unifying force in labor's frontal attack on capital in the ensuing class struggle (Beams 1998; Katz-Fishman et al. 2002).[3]

Imperialism today represents a dual, contradictory development whose dialectical resolution is an outcome of its very nature—a product of its growth and expansion across time and space within the confines of a structure that promotes its own destruction and demise. However, while the process itself is a self-destructing one, it is important to understand that the nature of the class struggle that these contradictions generate is such that the critical factor that tips the balance of class forces in favor of the proletariat to win state power is political organization, the building of class alliances among the oppressed and exploited classes, the development of strong and theoretically well-informed revolutionary leadership that is organically linked to the working class, and a clear understanding of the forces at work in the class struggle, including especially the role of the state and its military and police apparatus—the focal point of the struggle for state power (Szymanski 1978; Berberoglu 2001; Knapp and Spector 1991). The success of the working class and its revolutionary leadership in confronting the power of the state thus becomes the critical element ensuring that once captured, the state can become an instrument that the workers can use to establish their rule and in the process transform society and the state itself to promote proletarian interests in line with its vision for a new society free of exploitation and oppression, one based on the rule of the working class and the laboring masses in general.

Our understanding of the necessity for change and social transformation, which is political in nature, necessitates a clear, scientific understanding of modern imperialism in its late twentieth- and early twenty-first-century form so that this knowledge can be put to use to facilitate the class struggle in a revolutionary direction. In this context, one will want to know not only the extent and depth of global capitalist expansion, but also its base of support, its linkage to the major institutions of capitalist society (above all the state, but also other religious, cultural, and social institutions), the extent of its ideological hegemony and control over mass consciousness, and other aspects of social, economic, political, and ideological domination. Moreover—and this is the most important point—one must study its weaknesses, its problem areas, its vulnerabilities, its weak links, and the various dimensions of its crisis—especially those that affect its continued reproduction and survival. Armed with this knowledge, one would be better equipped to confront capital and the capitalist state in the struggle to transform imperialism and the globalization process that today, in the early twenty-first century, represents the highest and most mature stage of global capitalism.

CLASS STRUGGLE AND
SOCIAL TRANSFORMATION

Thanks to the growing literature on globalization and global capitalism, we now have a greater understanding of the structure of capitalist imperialism and its contradictions. We know, for example, the extent of global capitalist expansion, the nature of imperialist intervention around the world, and the various social, economic, and political contradictions of imperialism today (Szymanski 1981; Berberoglu 1987b; Petras and Veltmeyer 2001). These consist of:

1. The contradiction among the capitalists of various imperialist states (or interimperialist rivalry)
2. The contradiction between the capitalists of the various imperialist states and the workers in the Third World
3. The contradiction between the capitalists and the workers within the imperialist states
4. The contradiction between the capitalists of the imperialist states and the remaining socialist states and peoples' movements throughout the world

The question that one now confronts is a *political* one. Given what we know of imperialism and its class contradictions on a world scale, how will the peoples' movements respond to imperialism *politically* worldwide? What strategy and tactics will be adopted to confront this colossal force? It is important to think about these questions concretely, in a practical way—one that involves a concrete scientific analysis and organized political action.

One central location of this battleground has been the Third World, where efforts toward the development of solidarity among workers to build the basis of a true labor internationalism has been quite successful. Armed with proletarian solidarity, a rank-and-file international workers' movement mobilized across national boundaries has the potential to play a strong role in bringing together workers from various countries in their struggle against transnational capital and the global capitalist system. Such international solidarity among Third World workers could represent a mighty force in the struggle against imperialism and capitalist exploitation throughout the world (Howard 1995; Bina and Davis 2002).

Strikes, demonstrations, and mass protests initiated by workers and other popular forces have become frequent in a growing number of countries controlled by imperialism in recent years. The working people are rising up against the local ruling classes, the state, and the transnational monopolies that have together effected the superexploitation of labor for decades. Varied forms of class struggle on the one hand and the struggle for national liberation led by labor on the other are two sides of the same process of struggle for the transformation of society now underway in many countries under the grip of foreign capital.

The logic of transnational capitalist expansion on a global scale is such that it leads to the emergence and development of forces in conflict with this expansion. The working class has been in the forefront of these forces. And strikes, mass demonstrations, political protest, confrontation with the local client state machine, armed insurrection, civil war, and revolutionary upheavals are all part and parcel of the contradictory nature of relations imposed on the laboring people by imperialism and its client states throughout the Third World.

Another important location of this battleground is Europe. German imperialism is growing and expanding throughout Europe and the world. The danger stemming from this economic expansion is real, and as the decision to send German troops to the former Yugoslavia has shown, such expansion will increasingly take a political and military form to protect this expanding economic interest. However, the growing German influence in Europe has become a focal point of resistance against German and European imperialism throughout the continent as part of the effort directed at confronting the forces of globalization.

Yet another rallying point of struggle has been around the North American Free Trade Agreement and other neoliberal policies of U.S. imperialism within the United States itself. Here, it is important to note the protracted battle that has been waged against U.S. imperialism for its economic intervention in Mexico and elsewhere to dominate the Latin American economies. This has been an important effort on the part of labor to build solidarity between U.S.

and Mexican (and other Latin American) labor, progressive trade unions, and leftist political organizations in building links and alliances that can translate into concrete political action, including general strikes, demonstrations, and protests along the U.S.-Mexican border—action that represents the unified efforts of both U.S. and Mexican workers that have also been used to confront Mexican capital and the Mexican state, as well as U.S. transnationals and the U.S. imperial state.

All of these efforts have become important components of a much broader international solidarity of working people that is yet to develop between the workers of the Third World and workers in the advanced capitalist countries in North America, Europe, and elsewhere. Elements of this new emergent solidarity were seen in the recent protests and demonstrations in Seattle (in November 1999), Washington, D.C. (in April 2000), Prague (in September 2000), and several more recent protests in a number of cities in the United States, Canada, and Europe in 2001 and 2002, where labor has played an important role in building the basis of a solidarity across many groups that are allied in this struggle (Wallach and Sforza 2000; Starr 2001; Houtart and Polet 2001; Smith and Johnston 2002; Katsiaficas and Yuen 2002). And this alliance and struggle will surely grow and spread to many parts of the world in the years ahead.

Finally, another important arena of political struggle has been the building of solidarity with the remaining socialist states that have come under imperialist attack. This has included support of movements that are struggling to defeat the reactionary, procapitalist forces in Eastern Europe and the former Soviet Union in order to build a new type of socialist society that is based on the working class and led by the workers themselves.

Together, these struggles have been effective in frustrating the efforts of imperialism to expand and dominate the world, while at the same time building the basis of an international working-class movement that finally overcomes national, ethnic, cultural, and linguistic boundaries that artificially separate the workers in their fight against imperialism. The solidarity achieved through this process has helped expand the strength of the international working class and increased its determination to defeat imperialism and all vestiges of global capitalism throughout the world and build a new egalitarian world social order that advances the interests of the working people and ultimately all of humanity.

NOTES

1. This paradox of growth and expansion of capital on a world scale, simultaneously with the decline and contraction of the domestic economy, is a central feature

of globalization and imperialism at its highest and most intense stage of worldwide capitalist expansion.

2. While one consequence of imperialism and globalization has been economic contraction and an associated class polarization, a more costly and dangerous outcome of this process has been increased militarization and intervention abroad, such that the defense of an expanding capitalist empire worldwide has come to require an increasing military presence and a permanent interventionist foreign policy to keep the world economy clear of obstructions that go against the interests of the transnational monopolies. However, such aggressive military posture has had (and continues to create) major problems for the imperialist state and is increasingly threatening its effectiveness and, in the long run, its very existence.

3. The necessity of the struggle against global capital in an organized political fashion has been emphasized by working-class organizations throughout the twentieth century following the successful Russian Revolution led by Lenin in 1917. Since then, the political organs of the working class have emphasized the centrality of international working-class solidarity (or proletarian internationalism) for any worldwide effort to wage a successful battle against global capitalism.

Conclusion

Today, in this first decade of the twenty-first century, the globalization of capital has reached its apex and encompasses every corner of the world. The domination of the world economy by a handful of transnational corporations supported by their imperial states has facilitated the transformation of entire societies into capitalist ones, where capitalist relations of production have replaced traditional precapitalist relations, incorporating these societies into the world economy dominated by the transnationals. Through this process, the transnational corporations of the imperialist states have turned much of the world's population into a superexploited mass of wage-laborers for the sole purpose of profit for the owners of these corporations.

I have shown throughout this book the centrality of the contradictions that the globalization of capital has generated through the logic of capital accumulation on a world scale. I have argued that globalization (or the global expansion of transnational monopoly capital) is the highest and most intensive and accelerated stage of modern imperialism. This is so because capitalism, having reached its most mature stage, has spread to the remote corners of the world and has come to dominate vast territories in which millions of working people have become enslaved to the dictates of capital propped up by the capitalist/imperialist state.

During the twentieth century, especially after World War II, U.S. capital came to play a prominent role in the world economy and dominated the capitalist world in the postwar period, leading to its rise onto the world scene in direct competition to its European and East Asian rivals. While this has resulted in greater interimperialist conflict and rivalry between the contending capitalist powers, sometimes leading to open warfare, the U.S. imperial state has played a central role in protecting and advancing the interests of U.S. capital across the world.

The process of imperialist expansion through globalization, however, has its own contradictions at the national and international levels. As I have shown in numerous places in this book, globalization, imperialism, and capital accumulation on a world scale have led to the exploitation of the great majority of the world's population. In addition to direct economic exploitation of wage-labor worldwide, the globalization of capital through this process has intensified repression of the working class by the Third World capitalist state, and this in turn has led to greater instability, conflict, and struggle against capital and the capitalist state throughout the world.

On another level, the maintenance of a global empire has necessitated the expansion of the powers of the imperial state around the world. This has taken the form of military intervention and domination through a variety of political-military mechanisms of control. The imperial state in this way has been successful, at least thus far, to ward off any threat against capital and the global capitalist system. While this has been a costly affair for both the state and the public who have paid a heavy price both in lives and dollars, the ultimate success of the imperial state to crush its enemies, even at a high cost to its own people, has yielded for transnational capital its prominent place in the world economy and polity to dictate its terms. This process of global domination of capital and the imperial state has been made possible by the collaboration of the capitalist state in the Third World, which has come to play a supportive, neocolonial role to foster transnational capitalist expansion—one from which the Third World state reaps substantial benefits through foreign military aid from the imperial center designed to keep civilian and military dictatorships in power in order to facilitate the transnational capitalist accumulation process.

While the primary economic contradiction of globalization has been the exploitation of wage-labor by capital on a world scale, and this has necessitated worldwide domination and repression of the working class and plunder of less developed capitalist societies around the world, a secondary but an important contradiction of this process has been domestic economic decline in the United States. I have examined this problem as a manifestation of the globalization of U.S. capital that has sought to increase its profits manyfold through the export of capital to the Third World, where profit rates are much higher than at home. This has, in turn, brought about the decline of domestic industry and with it greater unemployment, decline in union membership, lowering of wages, and a general decline in the standard of living of the working class in the United States.

The political implications of these developments are such that an exploitative capitalist empire that has brought so much misery and destitution abroad is now inflicting more and more a similar level of misery on its own workers at home, such that increased exploitation of a global working class is now bringing together diverse segments of international labor to establish the basis of a global solidarity of workers for building a new transnational labor movement that will wage an effective struggle against global capital and win.

This is the heart of the matter when it comes to the analysis of the meaning of globalization and its contradictions. That is, globalization, in essence, ushers in a period of global struggle between labor and capital on a worldwide scale. And ultimately, it is a struggle for state power: for transnational capital to hold on to its power over the capitalist state and use it to advance its own class interests, and for the working class to struggle for and capture state power to establish and impose its class rule.

The underlying central theme of this book that runs through the various chapters has been an analysis of the dynamics and contradictions of globalization and imperialism, the role of the nation-state, and the struggle between labor and capital leading to open class conflict. To illustrate these and other related questions and their relationship to labor, capital, and the state, I have provided much data and analysis throughout the book to highlight the importance of revealing the nature and dynamics of the globalization process and its inherent contradictions. If, through this effort, I have succeeded in facilitating renewed discussion and debate on globalization and its logic as an advanced stage of imperialism with all its particular characteristics, then the forces at work that want to conceal the real nature and purpose of globalization can, through such debate, be exposed for what they are: the agents of capital accumulation, superexploitation, and worldwide imperialist domination. In fact, these are the end results of the machinations of global capitalism at work on a worldwide scale. What the future holds for the dominant forces of modern-day conquest and plunder that have imposed their class agenda onto the rest of the world, history and the working classes of the world will ultimately determine. And thus, it is not unreasonable to expect that, like everything else in history, the globalization of capital and the capitalist nation-state may in fact one day be a thing of the past!

Bibliography

Afshar, Haleh, and Stephanie Barrientos, eds. 1999. *Women, Globalization and Fragmentation in the Developing World.* Basingstoke: Macmillan.

Aglietta, Michel. 1982a. *Regulation and the Crisis of Capitalism.* New York: Monthly Review.

———. 1982b. "World Capitalism in the 1980s." *New Left Review* 136 (November–December).

Alexandrov, Sergei, et al., eds. 2001. *Afghanistan's Unknown War: Memoirs of Russian War Veterans.* Toronto: Megapolis.

Amaladoss, Michael, ed. 1999. *Globalization and Its Victims As Seen by Its Victims.* Delhi, India: Vidyajyoti Education and Welfare Society.

Amin, Samir. 1990a. *Delinking: Towards a Polycentric World.* London: Zed.

———. 1990b. *Maldevelopment: Anatomy of a Global Failure.* London: Zed.

———. 1997. *Capitalism in the Age of Globalization: The Management of Contemporary Society.* London: Zed.

———. 2001. "Imperialism and Globalization." *Monthly Review* 53, no. 2 (June).

Amoroso, Bruno. 2001. *On Globalization: Capitalism in the 21st Century.* New York: St. Martin's.

Appadurai, Arjun. 2001. *Globalization.* Durham, N.C.: Duke University Press.

Arrighi, Giovanni. 1994. *The Long Twentieth Century.* London: Verso.

Arrighi, Giovanni, and Beverly Silver. 1999. *Chaos and Governance in the Modern World-System.* Minneapolis: University of Minnesota Press.

Atal, Yogesh, ed. 1999. *Poverty in Transition and Transition in Poverty: Recent Developments in Hungary, Bulgaria, Romania Georgia, Russia, Mongolia.* New York: UN Educational Press.

Ayala, Cesar J. 1989. "Theories of Big Business in American Society." *Critical Sociology* 16, nos. 2–3 (Summer–Fall).

Bamyeh, Mohammed A. 2000. *The Ends of Globalization.* Minneapolis: University of Minnesota Press.

Baran, Paul A., and Paul M. Sweezy. 1966. *Monopoly Capital.* New York: Monthly Review.

Barkin, David. 1982. "Internationalization of Capital: An Alternative Approach." In *Dependency and Marxism,* ed. Ronald Chilcote. Boulder, Colo.: Westview.

Barkin, David, Irene Ortiz, and Fred Rosen. 1997. "Globalization and Resistance: The Remaking of Mexico." *NACLA* 30, no. 40.

Barndt, Deborah, ed. 1999. *Women Working the NAFTA Food Chain: Women, Food and Globalization.* Toronto: Sumach.

————. 2002. *Tangled Routes: Women, Work, and Globalization on the Tomato Trail.* Boulder, Colo.: Rowman and Littlefield.

Barnet, Richard J., and Ronald E. Muller. 1974. *Global Reach.* New York: Simon and Schuster.

Barnet, Richard, and John Cavenagh. 1994. *Global Dreams: Imperial Corporations and the New World Order.* New York: Simon and Schuster.

Bauman, Z. 1998. *Globalization: The Human Consequences.* Cambridge: Polity.

Beams, Nick. 1998. *The Significance and Implications of Globalization: A Marxist Assessment.* Southfield, UK: Mehring.

Bello, Walden, and Stephanie Rosenfeld. 1990. *Dragons in Distress: Asia's Miracle Economies in Crisis.* San Francisco: Institute for Food and Development Policy.

Beneria, Lourdes. 1989. "Gender and the Global Economy." In *Instability and Change in the World Economy,* ed. Arthur MacEwan and William K. Tabb. New York: Monthly Review.

Berberoglu, Berch. 1987a. "The Contradictions of Export-Oriented Development in the Third World." *Social and Economic Studies* 36, no. 4 (December).

————. 1987b. *The Internationalization of Capital: Imperialism and Capitalist Development on a World Scale.* New York: Praeger.

————. 1990. *Political Sociology: A Comparative/Historical Approach.* New York: General Hall.

————. 1992a. *The Legacy of Empire: Economic Decline and Class Polarization in the United States.* New York: Praeger.

————. 1992b. *The Political Economy of Development: Development Theory and the Prospects for Change in the Third World.* Albany: SUNY Press.

————. 1993. "The Political Economy of the Gulf War." *Humanity and Society* 17, no. 1.

————. 1994. *Class Structure and Social Transformation.* New York: Praeger.

————. 1996. "Imperialism and Class Struggle in the Late 20th Century." *Humanity and Society* 20, no. 2 (May).

————. 1999. *Turmoil in the Middle East: Imperialism, War, and Political Instability.* Boulder, Colo.: Rowman and Littlefield.

————. 2001. *Political Sociology: A Comparative/Historical Approach.* 2nd ed. New York: General Hall.

————, ed. 2002. *Labor and Capital in the Age of Globalization: The Labor Process and the Changing Nature of Work in the Global Economy.* Boulder, Colo.: Rowman and Littlefield.

Berger, Peter, and Samuel P. Huntington, eds. 2002. *Many Globalizations: Cultural Diversity in the Contemporary World.* New York: Oxford University Press.

Bergman, Gregory. 1986. "The 1920s and the 1980s: A Comparison." *Monthly Review* 38, no. 5 (October).

Bina, Cyrus, and Chuck Davis. 1996. "Wage Labor and Global Capital: Global Competition and the Universalization of the Labor Movement." In *Beyond Survival: Wage Labor in the Late Twentieth Century,* ed. Cyrus Bina et al. Armonk, N.Y.: Sharpe.

———. 2000. "Globalization, Technology, and Skill Formation in Capitalism." In *Political Economy and Contemporary Capitalism: Radical Perspectives on Economic Theory and Policy,* ed. Ron Baiman et al. Armonk, N.Y.: Sharpe.

———. 2002. "Dynamics of Globalization: Transnational Capital and the International Labor Movement." In *Labor and Capital in the Age of Globalization: The Labor Process and the Changing Nature of Work in the Global Economy,* ed. Berch Berberoglu. Boulder, Colo.: Rowman and Littlefield.

Bina, Cyrus, and Behzad Yaghmaian. 1991. "Post-war Global Accumulation and the Transnationalization of Capital." *Capital and Class,* no. 43 (Spring).

Biro, Lajos, and Marc J. Cohen, eds. 1979. *The United States in Crisis.* Minneapolis: MEP Press.

Black, Stanley W., ed. 1998. *Globalization, Technological Change, and Labor Markets.* Boston: Kluwer.

Block, Fred. 1977. "The Ruling Class Does Not Rule: Notes on the Marxist Theory of the State." *Socialist Review,* no. 33 (May–June).

———. 1978. "Class Consciousness and Capitalist Rationalization: A Reply to Critics." *Socialist Review,* nos. 40–41 (July–October).

Blomstrom, Magnus, and Bjorn Hettne. 1984. *Development Theory in Transition: Dependency Theory and Beyond.* London: Zed.

Bluestone, Barry, and Bennett Harrison. 1982. *The Deindustrialization of America.* New York: Basic.

Blum, William. 2001. *Rogue State: A Guide to the World's Only Superpower.* London: Zed.

Bonacich, Edna, Lucie Cheng, Norma Chinchilla, Nora Hamilton, and Paul Ong, eds. 1994. *Global Production: The Apparel Industry in the Pacific Rim.* Philadelphia: Temple University Press.

Bond, Patrick. 2002. "Zimbabwe, South Africa, and the Power Politics of Bourgeois Democracy." *Monthly Review* 54, no. 1 (May).

Bonosky, Phillip. 2001. *Afghanistan: Washington's Secret War.* 2nd ed. New York: International.

Boron, Atilio. 1995. *State, Capitalism, and Democracy in Latin America.* Boulder, Colo.: Rienner.

Borovik, Artyom. 2001. *The Hidden War: A Russian Journalist's Account of the Soviet War in Afghanistan.* New York: Grove.

Borrego, John, Alejandro Alvarez Bejar, and Jomo K. S., eds. 1996. *Capital, the State, and Late Industrialization.* Boulder, Colo.: Westview.

Bowles, Samuel, and Richard Edwards. 1985. *Understanding Capitalism.* New York: Harper and Row.

Boyd-Barrett, Oliver, and Terhi Rantanen, eds. 1998. *The Globalization of News.* Thousand Oaks, Calif.: Sage.

Boyer, Richard, and Herbert Morais. 1980. *Labor's Untold Story.* 3rd ed. New York: United Electrical, Radio, and Machine Workers of America.

Braun, Denny. 1991. *The Rich Get Richer: The Rise of Income Inequality in the United States and the World.* Chicago: Nelson-Hall.

Brecher, Jeremy, and Tim Costello. 1998. *Global Village or Global Pillage: Economic Reconstruction from the Bottom Up.* Cambridge, Mass.: South End.

Brenner, Robert. 1977. "The Origins of Capitalist Development: A Critique of Neo-Smithian Marxism." *New Left Review* 104.

——. 1991. "Why Is the United States at War with Iraq?" *New Left Review,* no. 185.

Bresheeth, Haim, and Nira Yuval-Davis, eds. 1991. *The Gulf War and the New World Order.* London: Zed.

Broad, Robin. 2002. *Global Backlash: Citizen Initiatives for a Just World Economy.* Boulder, Colo.: Rowman and Littlefield.

Brown, Jonathan C., ed. 1997. *Workers' Control in Latin America, 1930–1979.* Chapel Hill: University of North Carolina Press.

Brown, Michael Barratt. 1974. *The Economics of Imperialism.* Baltimore, Md.: Penguin.

Bryan, Dick. 1995a. *The Chase across the Globe: International Accumulation and the Contradictions for Nation States.* Boulder, Colo.: Westview.

——. 1995b. "The Internationalization of Capital and Marxian Value Theory." *Cambridge Journal of Economics* 19.

Burbach, Roger, and Ben Clarke, eds. 2002. *September 11 and the U.S. War: Beyond the Curtain of Smoke.* San Francisco: City Lights.

Burbach, Roger, Orlando Núñez, and Boris Kagarlitsky. 1996. *Globalization and Its Discontents: The Rise of Postmodern Socialisms.* London: Pluto.

——. 2001. *Globalization and Postmodern Politics.* London: Pluto.

Buxton, Julia, and Nicola Phillips, eds. 1999. *Case Studies in Latin American Political Economy.* Manchester, UK: Manchester University Press.

Calleo, David. 1987. *Beyond American Hegemony: The Future of the Western Alliance.* New York: Basic.

Callinicos, Alex. 1991. *The Revenge of History: Marxism and the East European Revolutions.* University Park: Pennsylvania State University Press.

Cammack, Paul. 1997. *Capitalism and Democracy in the Third World.* London: Leicester University.

Cantor, Daniel, and Juliet Schor. 1987. *Tunnel Vision: Labor, the World Economy, and Central America.* Boston: South End.

Cappo, Joe. 1977. "A Little Closer Look at Free Enterprise." *Chicago Daily News,* 17 May.

Cardoso, Fernando Henrique. 2001. *Charting a New Course: The Politics of Globalization and Social Transformation.* Boulder, Colo.: Rowman and Littlefield.

Cardoso, Fernando Henrique, and Enzo Faletto. 1979. *Dependency and Development in Latin America.* Berkeley: University of California Press.

Carnoy, Martin. 1984. *The State and Political Theory.* Princeton, N.J.: Princeton University Press.

Chandra, Bipan. 1975. "The Indian Capitalist Class and Imperialism Before 1947." *Journal of Contemporary Asia* 5, no. 3.

Chase-Dunn, Christopher. 1998. *Global Formation: Structures of the World Economy.* Boulder, Colo.: Rowman and Littlefield.

Chase-Dunn, Christopher, Susanne Jonas, and Nelson Amaro, eds. 2001. *Globalization on the Ground: Postbellum Guatemalan Democracy and Development.* Boulder, Colo.: Rowman and Littlefield.

Chattopadhyay, Paresh. 1992. "Some Trends in India's Capitalist Industrialization." In *Class, State and Development in India,* ed. Berch Berberoglu. New Delhi: Sage.

Cherry, Robert, et al., eds. 1987. *The Imperiled Economy.* Bk. 1. New York: Union for Radical Political Economics.

Chilcote, Ronald H., ed. 1982. *Dependency and Marxism: Toward a Resolution of the Debate.* Boulder, Colo.: Westview.

Clapp, Jennifer. 2001. *Toxic Exports: The Transfer of Hazardous Wastes from Rich to Poor Countries.* Ithaca, N.Y.: Cornell University Press.

Clark, Gordon L., and Won Bae Kim, eds. 1995. *Asian NIEs and the Global Economy: Industrial Restructuring and Corporate Strategy in the 1990s.* Baltimore, Md.: Johns Hopkins University Press.

Clark, Robert P. 2001. *Global Life Systems: Population, Food, and Disease in the Process of Globalization.* Boulder, Colo.: Rowman and Littlefield.

———. 2002. *Global Awareness: Thinking Systematically about the World.* Boulder, Colo.: Rowman and Littlefield.

Clawson, Patrick. 1977. "The Internationalization of Capital and Capital Accumulation in Iran and Iraq." *Insurgent Sociologist* 7, no. 2 (Spring).

Cockcroft, James D. 1996. *Latin America: History, Politics, and U.S. Policy.* 2nd ed. Belmont, Calif.: Wadsworth.

Cohn, Theodore H., Stephen McBride, and John Wiseman, eds. 2000. *Power in the Global Era: Grounding Globalization.* New York: St. Martin's.

Collins, Susan M., ed. 1998. *Imports, Exports, and the American Worker.* Washington, D.C.: Brookings.

Comeliau, Christian. 2002. *The Impasse of Modernity: Debating the Future of the Global Market Economy.* London: Zed.

Cornwell, Grant H., and Eve Walsh Stoddard, eds. 2000. *Global Multiculturalism: Comparative Perspectives on Ethnicity, Race, and Nation.* Boulder, Colo.: Rowman and Littlefield.

Cuyvers, Ludo. 2001. *Globalisation and Social Development: European and Southeast Asian Evidence.* Cheltenham, UK: Edward Elgar.

Dadush, Uri B., Dipak Dasgupta, and Marc Uzan, eds. 2001. *Private Capital Flows in the Age of Globalization: The Aftermath of the Asian Crisis.* Cheltenham, UK: Edward Elgar.

Danaher, Kevin, and Roger Burbach, eds. 2000. *Globalize This! The Battle against the World Trade Organization and Corporate Rule.* Monroe, Maine: Common Courage.

Davidson, Basil. 1961. *The African Slave Trade.* Boston: Little, Brown.

Davis, Mike. 1984. "The Political Economy of Late Imperial America." *New Left Review* 143 (January–February).

De Caux, Len. 1970. *Labor Radical.* Boston: Beacon.

———. 1974. "UE: Democratic Unionism at Work." *World Magazine* (April).

Desai, A. R. 1984. *India's Path of Development.* Bombay: Popular Prakashan.

Devine, Jim. 1982. "The Structural Crisis of U.S. Capitalism." *Southwest Economy and Society* 6, no. 1 (Fall).

Deyo, Frederick, Stephen Heggard, and Hagen Koo. 1987. "Labor in the Political Economy of East Asian Industrialization." *Bulletin of Concerned Asian Scholars* 19, no. 2 (April–June).

Dicken, Peter. 1992. *Global Shift: The Internationalization of Economic Activity.* New York: Guilford.

Dickenson, Torry D., and Robert K. Schaeffer. 2001. *Fast Forward: Work, Gender, and Protest in a Changing World.* Boulder, Colo.: Rowman and Littlefield.

Domhoff, G. William. 1998. *Who Rules America? Power and Politics in the Year 2000.* Mountain View, Calif.: Mayfield.

Dowd, Douglas F. 1977. *The Twisted Dream: Capitalist Development in the United States since 1776.* Cambridge, Mass.: Winthrop.

Dupuy, Alex. 1988. *Haiti in the World Economy: Class, Race, and Underdevelopment since 1700.* Boulder, Colo.: Westview.

Eckstein, Susan, ed. 2001. *Power and Popular Protest: Latin American Social Movements.* Berkeley: University of California Press.

Edoho, Felix Moses, ed. 1997. *Globalization and the New World Order: Promises, Problems, and Prospects for Africa in the Twenty-first Century.* Westport, Conn.: Praeger.

Edwards, Michael, and John Gaventa, eds. 2001. *Global Citizen Action.* Boulder, Colo.: Rienner.

Elbakidze, Marina, ed. 2002. *Globalization: A Bibliography with Indexes.* New York: Nova Science.

Elliott, Michael. 2002. "Special Report: The Secret History—They Had a Plan." *Time,* 12 August.

Emigh, Rebecca Jean, and Ivan Szelenyi, eds. 2000. *Poverty, Ethnicity, and Gender in Eastern Europe during the Market transition.* New York: Praeger.

Engardio, Pete. 2000. "Special Report: Global Capitalism." *Business Week,* 6 November.

Esping-Andersen, Gosta, Roger Friedland, and Erik Olin Wright. 1976. "Modes of Class Struggle and the Capitalist State." *Kapitalistate,* nos. 4–5 (Summer).

Falk, Richard. 1999. *Predatory Globalization: A Critique.* Malden, Mass.: Blackwell.

Fantasia, Rick. 1988. *Cultures of Solidarity: Consciousness, Action, and Contemporary American Workers.* Berkeley: University of California Press.

Fleming, D. F. 1961. *The Cold War and Its Origins, 1917–1960.* 2 vols. New York: Doubleday.

Foran, John, ed. 2002. *The Future of Revolutions: Rethinking Political and Social Change in the Age of Globalization.* London: Zed.

Fortune. 1989. 119, no. 9 (April 24).

———. 2002. 145, no. 8 (April 15).

Foster, John B. 1986. *The Theory of Monopoly Capitalism.* New York: Monthly Review.

———. 2001. "Imperialism and 'Empire.'" *Monthly Review* 53, no. 7 (December).

———. 2002. "Monopoly Capital and the New Globalization." *Monthly Review* 53, no. 8 (January).

Foster, John B., and Henryk Szlajfer, eds. 1984. *The Faltering Economy: The Problem of Accumulation under Monopoly Capitalism.* New York: Monthly Review.

Frank, Andre Gunder. 1967. *Capitalism and Underdevelopment in Latin America.* New York: Monthly Review.

———. 1975. *On Capitalist Underdevelopment.* Bombay: Oxford University Press.

French, Hilary F. 2000. *Vanishing Borders: Protecting the Planet in the Age of Globalization.* New York: Norton.

Friedman, Jonathan, ed. 2002. *Globalization, the State, and Violence.* Boulder, Colo.: Rowman and Littlefield.

Friedman, Kajsa Ekholm, and Jonathan Friedman. 2002. *Global Anthropology.* Boulder, Colo.: Rowman and Littlefield.

Fuentes, Annette, and Barbara Ehrenreich. 1983. *Women in the Global Factory.* Boston: South End.

Furtado, Celso. 1970. *Economic Development of Latin America.* London: Cambridge University Press.

Gerstein, Ira. 1977. "Theories of the World Economy and Imperialism." *Insurgent Sociologist* 7, no. 2 (Spring).

Giddens, Anthony. 2000. *Runaway World: How Globalization Is Reshaping Our Lives.* New York: Routledge.

Gills, Barry K. 2001. *Globalization and the Politics of Resistance.* New York: Palgrave Macmillan.

Gimenez, Martha. 1987. "The Feminization of Poverty: Myth or Reality." *The Insurgent Sociologist* 14, no. 3 (Fall).

Gohari, M. J. 2001. *The Taliban: Ascent to Power.* New York: Oxford University Press.

Gold, David, Clarence Y. H. Lo, and Erik Olin Wright. 1985. "Recent Developments in Marxist Theories of the Capitalist State." *Monthly Review* 27, nos. 5–6 (October–November).

Golding, Peter, and Phil Harris, eds. 1997. *Beyond Cultural Imperialism: Globalization, Communication and the New International Order.* Thousand Oaks, Calif.: Sage.

Goodson, Larry P. 2001. *Afghanistan's Endless War: State Failure, Regional Politics, and the Rise of the Taliban.* Seattle: University of Washington Press.

Green, Felix. 1971. *The Enemy: What Every American Should Know about Imperialism.* New York: Vintage.

Green, Gil. 1976. *What's Happening to Labor.* New York: International.

Greer, Edward. 1991."The Hidden History of the Iraq War." *Monthly Review* 43, no. 1.

Griffen, Sarah. 1991. "The War Bill: Adding up the Domestic Costs of War." *Dollars and Sense,* no. 165 (April).

Griffin, Keith, and Rahman Khan. 1992. *Globalisation and the Developing World: An Essay on the International Dimensions of Development in the Post–Cold War Era.* Geneva: UN Research Institute for Social Development.

Grosfoguel, Ramon, and Ana Cervantes-Rodriguez, eds. 2002. *The Modern/Colonial Capitalist World-System in the Twentieth Century: Global Processes, Antisystemic Movements, and the Geopolitics of Knowledge.* Westport, Conn.: Greenwood.

Gulalp, Haldun. 1983. "Frank and Wallerstein Revisited: A Contribution to Brenner's Critique." In *Neo-Marxist Theories of Development,* ed. Peter Limqueco and Bruce McFarlane. New York: St. Martin's.

Halebsky, Sander, and Richard L. Harris, eds. 1995. *Capital, Power, and Inequality in Latin America.* Boulder, Colo.: Westview.

Halevi, Joseph. 2002. "The Argentine Crisis." *Monthly Review* 53, no. 11 (April).

Halevi, Joseph, and Bill Lucarelli. 2002. "Japan's Stagnationist Crises." *Monthly Review* 53, no. 9 (February).

Hall, Burton, ed. 1972. *Autocracy and Insurgency in Organized Labor.* New Brunswick, N.J.: Transaction.

Halliday, Fred. 1979. *Iran: Dictatorship and Development.* New York: Penguin.

——. 2001. *The World at 2000.* New York: St. Martin's.

Halliday, John, and Gavan McCormic. 1973. *Japanese Imperialism Today.* New York: Monthly Review.

Hamilton, Clive. 1983. "Capitalist Industrialization in East Asia's Four Little Tigers." *Journal of Contemporary Asia* 13, no. 1.

——. 1986. *Capitalist Industrialization in Korea.* Boulder, Colo.: Westview.

Hamilton, Nora, and Timothy F. Harding, eds. 1986. *Modern Mexico: State, Economy, and Social Conflict.* Thousand Oaks, Calif.: Sage.

Hardt, Michael, and Antonio Negri. 2000. *Empire.* Cambridge, Mass.: Harvard University Press.

Harris, Richard, ed. 1975. *The Political Economy of Africa.* Cambridge, Mass.: Schenkman.

Harrison, Bennett, and Barry Bluestone. 1988. *The Great U-Turn: Corporate Restructuring and the Polarizing of America.* New York: Basic.

Hart, Jeffrey A. 1992. *Rival Capitalists: International Competitiveness in the United States, Japan, and Western Europe.* Ithaca, N.Y.: Cornell University Press.

Hart-Landsberg, Martin. 1993. *Rush to Development: Economic Change and Political Struggle in South Korea.* New York: Monthly Review.

Harvey, David. 1982. *The Limits to Capital.* Chicago: University of Chicago Press.

Hassan, Salah S., and Erdener Kaynak, eds. 1994. *Globalization of Consumer Markets: Structures and Strategies.* New York: International Business.

Haugerud, Angelique, M. Priscilla Stone, and Peter D. Little, eds. 2000. *Commodities and Globalization.* Boulder, Colo.: Rowman and Littlefield.

Headley, Bernard. 1991. "The 'New World Order' and the Persian Gulf War." *Humanity and Society* 15, no. 3.

Hedley, R. Alan. 2002. *Running out of Control: Dilemmas of Globalization.* West Hartford, Conn.: Kumarian.

Held, David, Anthony G. McGrew, David Goldblatt, and Jonathan Perraton. 1999. *Global Transformations: Politics, Economics, and Culture.* Palo Alto, Calif.: Stanford University Press.

Herold, Marc. 2002. "Who Will Count the Dead? Civilian Casualties in Afghanistan." In *September 11 and the U.S. War: Beyond the Curtain of Smoke,* ed. Roger Burbach and Ben Clarke. San Francisco: City Lights.

Hertz, Noreena. 2002. *Silent Takeover: Global Capitalism and the Death of Democracy.* New York: The Free Press.

Higgott, Richard A., and Anthony Payne, eds. 2000. *The New Political Economy of Globalisation.* Cheltenham, UK: Edward Elgar.

Hobson, John A. [1905] 1972. *Imperialism: A Study.* Rev. ed. Ann Arbor: University of Michigan Press.

Holloway, John. 1994. "Transnational Capital and the National State." *Capital and Class* 52.

Holzhausen, Arne, ed. 2001. *Can Japan Globalize?: Studies on Japan's Changing Political Economy and the Process of Globalization in Honour of Sung-Jo Park.* New York: Physica-Verlag.

Hoogvelt, Ankie M. M. 1982. *The Third World in Global Development.* London: Macmillan.

Hook, Glenn D., and Hasegawa Harukiyo, eds. 2001. *Political Economy of Japanese Globalization.* New York: Routledge.

Hopkins, Terence K., and Immanuel Wallerstein. 1981. "Structural Transformations of the World-Economy." In *Dynamics of World Development,* ed. Richard Rubinson. Beverly Hills, Calif.: Sage.

Houtart, François, and François Polet, eds. 2001. *The Other Davos Summit: The Globalization of Resistance to the World Economic System.* London: Zed.

Howard, Andrew. 1995. "Global Capital and Labor Internationalism in Comparative Historical Perspective: A Marxist Analysis." *Sociological Inquiry* 65, nos. 3–4 (November).

Howe, Carolyn. 1986. "The Politics of Class Compromise in an International Context: Considerations for a New Strategy for Labor." *Review of Radical Political Economics* 18, no. 3.

Howe, Irving, ed. 1972. *The World of the Blue Collar Worker.* New York: Quadrangle.

Hudson, Yeager, ed. 1999. *Globalism and the Obsolescence of the State.* Lewiston, N.Y.: Mellen.

Hurrell, Andrew, ed. 1999. *Inequality, Globalization, and World Politics.* New York: Oxford University Press.

Hutton, Will, and Anthony Giddens, eds. 2000. *Global Capitalism.* New York: The New Press.

Institute for Labor Education and Research. 1982. *What's Wrong with the U.S. Economy?* Boston: South End.

International Labour Office. 1998. *Yearbook of Labour Statistics, 1998.* Geneva: International Labor Office.

International Monetary Fund. Various Years. *Direction of Trade Statistics, Yearbook.* Washington, D.C.: International Monetary Fund.

James, Harold. 2002. *The End of Globalization: Lessons from the Great Depression.* Cambridge, Mass.: Harvard University Press.

Jenkins, Craig, and C. Eckert. 1989. "The Corporate Elite, the New Conservative Policy Network, and Reaganomics." *Critical Sociology* 16, nos. 2–3 (Summer–Fall).

Jonas, Susanne. 1991. *The Battle for Guatemala: Rebels, Death Squads, and U.S. Power.* Boulder, Colo.: Westview.

Jones, R. J. Barry. 2000. *The World Turned upside Down? Globalization and the Future of the State.* Manchester: Manchester University Press.

Jung, Hwa Yol, ed. 2002. *Comparative Political Culture in the Age of Globalization.* Boulder, Colo.: Rowman and Littlefield.

Kagarlitsky, Boris. 2000. *The Twilight of Globalization: Property, State, and Capitalism.* London: Pluto.

Kalb, Don, Marco Van Der Land, Richard Staring, and Nico Wilterdink, eds. 2000. *The Ends of Globalization: Bringing Society Back In.* Boulder, Colo.: Rowman and Littlefield.

Kang, David C. 2002. *Crony Capitalism: Corruption and Development in South Korea and the Philippines.* Cambridge: Cambridge University Press.

Kapstein, Ethan B. 1999. *Sharing the Wealth: Workers and the World Economy.* New York: Norton.

Karliner, Joshua. 1997. *The Corporate Planet: Ecology and Politics in the Age of Globalization.* Los Angeles: University of California Press.

Katsiaficas, George, and Eddie Yuen, eds. 2002. *The Battle of Seattle: Debating Capitalist Globalization and the WTO.* New York: Soft Skull.

Katz-Fishman, Walda, et al. 2002. "Globalization of Capital and Class Struggle." In *Labor and Capital in the Age of Globalization: The Labor Process and the Changing Nature of Work in the Global Economy,* ed. Berch Berberoglu. Boulder, Colo.: Rowman and Littlefield.

Katznelson, Ira, and Aristide R. Zolberg, eds. 1986. *Working-Class Formation: Nineteenth-Century Patterns in Western Europe and the United States.* Princeton, N.J.: Princeton University Press.

Kay, Cristobal. 1989. *Latin American Theories of Development and Underdevelopment.* London: Routledge and Kegan Paul.

Keeran, Roger. 1980. *The Communist Party and the Auto Workers' Unions.* Bloomington: Indiana University Press.

Kelly, Rita Mae, Jane H. Bayes, Mary Hawkesworth, and Brigitte Young, eds. 2001. *Gender, Globalization, and Democratization.* Boulder, Colo.: Rowman and Littlefield.

Kennedy, Paul. 1987. *The Rise and Fall of the Great Powers.* New York: Random House.

Kennedy, Paul, Dirk Messner, and Franz Nuscheler, eds. 2002. *Global Trends and Global Governance.* London: Pluto.

Khor, Martin. 2001. *Rethinking Globalization.* London: Zed.

Kidron, Michael. 1970. *Western Capitalism since the War.* Rev. ed. Harmondsworth, UK: Penguin.

Kim, Samuel S., ed. 2000. *East Asia and Globalization.* Boulder, Colo.: Rowman and Littlefield.

Kim, Sueng-Kyung. 1997. *Class Struggle or Family Struggle?: The Lives of Women Factory Workers in South Korea.* Cambridge: Cambridge University Press.

Kimeldorf, Howard. 1988. *Reds or Rackets? The Making of Radical and Conservative Unions on the Waterfront.* Berkeley: University of California Press.

Klak, Thomas, ed. 1997. *Globalization and Neoliberalism.* Boulder, Colo.: Rowman and Littlefield.

Kloby, Jerry. 1987. "The Growing Divide: Class Polarization in the 1980s." *Monthly Review* 39, no. 4 (September).

———. 1988. "The Top-Heavy Economy: Managerial Greed and Unproductive Labor." *Critical Sociology* 15, no. 3 (Fall).

———. 1993. "Increasing Class Polarization in the United States: The Growth of Wealth and Income Inequality." In *Critical Perspectives in Sociology: A Reader,* ed. Berch Berberoglu. Dubuque, Iowa: Kendall/Hunt.

Knapp, Peter, and Alan J. Spector. 1991. *Crisis and Change: Basic Questions of Marxist Sociology.* Chicago: Nelson-Hall.

Knowlton, Christopher, and Carla Rapoport. 1991. "Germany and Japan: Missing in Action." *Fortune* (March 11).

Kotovsky, G. 1992. "The Origins and Development of the Communist and Workers' Movement in India, with Focus on the CPI." In *Class, State, and Development in India,* ed. Berch Berberoglu. Delhi: Sage.

Kozul-Wright, Richard, and Robert Rowthorn, eds. 1998. *Transnational Corporations and the Global Economy.* New York: St. Martin's.

Landsberg, Martin. 1979. "Export-Led Industrialization in the Third World: Manufacturing Imperialism." *Review of Radical Political Economics* 11, no. 4 (Winter).

———. 1988. "South Korea: The 'Miracle' Rejected." *Critical Sociology* 15, no. 3.

Larrain, Jorge. 1989. *Theories of Development: Capitalism, Colonialism, and Dependency.* Cambridge: Polity.

Larrowe, Charles P. 1972. Harry Bridges. *The Rise and Fall of Radical Labor in the U.S.* Westport, Conn.: Lawrence Hill.

Lechner, Frank J., and John Boli, eds. 1999. *The Globalization Reader.* Oxford: Blackwell.

Lembcke, Jerry. 1988. *Capitalist Development and Class Capacities: Marxist Theory and Union Organization.* Westport, Conn.: Greenwood.

Lenin, V. I. [1917] 1975. *Imperialism: The Highest Stage of Capitalism. Selected Works.* Vol. 1. Moscow: Foreign Languages Publishing House.

Levenstein, Harvey. 1981. *Communism, Anticommunism, and the CIO.* Westport, Conn.: Greenwood.

Levine, Marvin J. 1997. *Worker Rights and Labor Standards in Asia's Four New Tigers: A Comparative Perspective.* New York: Plenum.

Levkovsky, A. I. 1966. *Capitalism in India.* Delhi: People's Publishing House.

Lewis, Cleona. 1938. *America's Stake in International Investments.* Washington, D.C.: Brookings.

Leys, Colin. 1977. "Underdevelopment and Dependency: Critical Notes." *Journal of Contemporary Asia* 7, no. 1.

Limqueco, Peter, and Bruce McFarlane, eds. 1983. *Neo-Marxist Theories of Development.* New York: St. Martin's.

Lindsey, Charles W. 1985. "The Philippine Economy." *Monthly Review* 36, no. 11 (April).

Lofdahl, Corey L. 2002. *Environmental Impacts of Globalization and Trade.* Cambridge: MIT Press.

Lotta, Raymond. 1984. *America in Decline.* Vol. 1. Chicago: Banner.

Luxemburg, Rosa. [1913] 1951. *The Accumulation of Capital.* Reprint. New Haven, Conn.: Yale University Press.

Magdoff, Harry. 1969. *The Age of Imperialism.* New York: Monthly Review.

———. 1978. *Imperialism: From the Colonial Age to the Present.* New York: Monthly Review.

———. 1992. *Globalization: To What End?* New York: Monthly Review.

Magdoff, Harry, and Paul M. Sweezy. 1977. *The End of Prosperity: The American Economy in the 1970s.* New York: Monthly Review.

———. 1981. *The Deepening Crisis of U.S. Capitalism.* New York: Monthly Review.

———. 1987. *Stagnation and the Financial Explosion.* New York: Monthly Review.

Mahajan, Rahul. 2002. *The New Crusade: America's War on Terrorism.* New York: Monthly Review.

Mahjoub, Azzam, ed. 1990. *Adjustment or Delinking? The African Experience.* London: Zed.

Maitra, Priyatosh. 1996. *The Globalization of Capitalism in Third World Countries.* Westport, Conn.: Praeger.

Mandel, Ernest. 1975. *Late Capitalism.* London: New Left.

———. 1980. *The Second Slump.* London: Verso.

Manser, Roger. 1994. *Failed Transitions: The Eastern European Economy and Environment Since the Fall of Communism.* New York: The New Press.

Marsden, Peter. 2002. *The Taliban: War and Religion in Afghanistan.* Rev. ed. London: Zed.

Martin, Hans-Peter, and Harold Schumann. 1997. *The Global Trap.* London: Zed.

Martin, Linda Grant. 1975. "The 500: A Report on Two Decades." *Fortune* (May).

Marx, Karl. [1853] 1986. "Future Results of the British Rule in India." In *India: National Liberation and Class Struggle,* ed. Berch Berberoglu. Meerut: Sarup and Sons.

Mayer, Tom. 1991. "Imperialism and the Gulf War." *Monthly Review* 42, no. 11.

Mayorga, Rene Antonio. 1978. "National-Popular State, State Capitalism and Military Dictatorship." *Latin American Perspectives* 5, no. 2.

McBride, Stephen, and John Wiseman, eds. 2000. *Globalization and Its Discontents.* New York: Palgrave Macmillan.

McMichael, Philip, et al. 1974. "Imperialism and the Contradictions of Development." *New Left Review* 85 (May–June).

McNally, David. 1991. "Beyond Nationalism, beyond Protectionism: Labor and the Canada-U.S. Free Trade Agreement." *Capital and Class,* no. 43 (Spring).

———. 1998. "Globalization on Trial: Crisis and Class Struggle in East Asia." In *Rising from the Ashes?: Labor in the Age of "Global" Capitalism,* ed. Ellen Meiksins Wood et al. New York: Monthly Review.

Medlen, Craig. 1984. "Corporate Taxes and the Federal Deficit." *Monthly Review* 36, no. 6 (November).

Meiksins Wood, Ellen, Peter Meiksins, and Michael Yates, eds. 1998. *Rising from the Ashes?: Labor in the Age of "Global" Capitalism.* New York: Monthly Review.

Melendez, Edwin. 1988. "Reaganomics and Racial Inequality: A Decade of Lost Gains." *Dollars and Sense,* no. 137 (June).

Melman, Seymour. 1965. *Our Depleted Society.* New York: Holt, Rinehart and Winston.

———. 1970. *Pentagon Capitalism: The Political Economy of War.* New York: McGraw-Hill.

Mermelstein, David, ed. 1975. *The Economic Crisis Reader.* New York: Vintage.

Meurs, Mieke. 1989. "Uncertain Harvest: The Making of the Next Farm Crisis." *Dollars and Sense,* no. 147 (June).

Meyer, Mary K., and Elisabeth Prügl, eds. 1999. *Gender Politics in Global Governance.* Boulder, Colo.: Rowman and Littlefield.

Milani, Brian. 2000. *Designing the Green Economy: The Post-industrial Alternative to Corporate Globalization.* Boulder, Colo.: Rowman and Littlefield.

Miles, Maria. 1990. *Patriarchy and Accumulation on a World Scale: Women in the International Division of Labor.* London: Zed.

Miller, John A. 1987. "Accumulation and State Intervention in the 1980s: A Crisis of Reproduction." In *The Imperiled Economy.* Bk. 1. Ed. Robert Cherry et al. New York: Union for Radical Political Economics.

Mittleman, James H., ed. 1996. *Globalization: Critical Reflections.* Boulder, Colo.: Rienner.

———. 2000. *The Globalization Syndrome: Transformation and Resistance.* Princeton, N.J.: Princeton University Press.

Mittelman, James H., and Norani Othman, eds. 2002. *Capturing Globalization.* New York: Routledge.

Mol, Arthur P. J. 2001. *Globalization and Environmental Reform.* Cambridge: MIT Press.

Moody, Kim. 1988. *An Injury to All: The Decline of American Unionism.* London: Verso.

———. 1990. "The Bad Deal: Bargaining in the 1980's." *Labor Notes,* no. 130 (January).

———. 1997. *Workers in a Lean World: Unions in the International Economy.* London: Verso.

Morris, George. 1971. *Rebellion in the Unions.* New York: New Outlook.

Morris, Nancy, and Silvio Waisbord. 2001. *Media and Globalization: Why the State Matters.* Boulder, Colo.: Rowman and Littlefield.

Moulder, Frances V. 1977. *Japan, China and the Modern World Economy.* Cambridge: Cambridge University Press.

Munck, Ronaldo. 1984. *Politics and Dependency in the Third World.* London: Zed.

———. 2002. *Globalization and Labor: The New Great Transformation.* London: Zed.

Munck, Ronaldo, and Peter Waterman, eds. 1999. *Labour Worldwide in the Era of Globalization: Alternative Union Models in the New World Order.* New York: Palgrave Macmillan.

Nabudere, Dan. 1977. *The Political Economy of Imperialism.* London: Zed.

———. 1981. *Imperialism in East Africa.* 2 Vols. London: Zed.

Nash, Andrew. 1999. "Mandela's Democracy." *Monthly Review* 50, no. 11 (April).

Nathanson, Charles E. 1969. "The Militarization of the American Economy." In *Corporations and the Cold War,* ed. David Horowitz. New York: Monthly Review.

Nayar, Baldev Raj. 2001. *Globalization and Nationalism: The Changing Balance in India's Economic Policy, 1950–2000.* Thousand Oaks, Calif.: Sage.

Nissen, Bruce. 1981. "U.S. Workers and the U.S. Labor Movement." *Monthly Review* 33, no. 1 (May).

———, ed. 2002. *Unions in a Globalized Environment: Changing Borders, Organizational Boundaries, and Social Roles.* Armonk, N.Y.: Sharpe.

Nojumi, Neamatollah. 2002. *The Rise of the Taliban in Afghanistan: Mass Mobilization, Civil War, and the Future of the Region.* New York: Palgrave Macmillan.

O'Brien, Philip. 1973. "Dependency: The New Nationalism?" In *Latin America Review of Books,* ed. Colin Harding and Christopher Roper. Palo Alto, Calif.: Ramparts.

O'Connor, James. 1973. *The Fiscal Crisis of the State.* New York: St. Martin's.

———. 1974. *The Corporations and the State.* New York: Harper and Row.

———. 1984. *Accumulation Crisis.* New York: Basil Blackwell.

O'Donnell, Guillermo. 1973. *Modernization and Bureaucratic Authoritarianism: Studies in South American Politics.* Berkeley: Institute of International Studies, University of California.

———. 1979. "Tensions in the Bureaucratic Authoritarian State and the Question of Democracy." In *The New Authoritarianism in Latin America,* ed. David Collier. Princeton, N.J.: Princeton University Press.

Olson, W. 1985. "Crisis and Social Change in Mexico's Political Economy." *Latin American Perspectives* 46.

O'Meara, Patrick, Howard Mehlinger, and Matthew Krain, eds. 2000. *Globalization and the Challenges of a New Century: A Reader.* Bloomington: Indiana University Press.

Owen, Roger, and Bob Sutcliffe, eds. 1972. *Studies in the Theory of Imperialism.* London: Longman.

Oxaal, Ivar, Tony Barnett, and David Booth, eds. 1975. *Beyond the Sociology of Development.* London: Routledge and Kegan Paul.

Palast, Greg. 2002. *The Best Democracy Money Can Buy: An Investigative Reporter Exposes the Truth about Globalization, Corporate Cons, and High Finance Fraudsters.* London: Pluto.

Panitch, Leo, and Colin Leys, eds. 1999. *Global Capitalism versus Democracy.* New York: Monthly Review.

Parenti, Michael. 1989. *The Sword and the Dollar: Imperialism, Revolution, and the Arms Race.* New York: St. Martin's.

———. 1995. *Against Empire.* San Francisco: City Lights.

———. 2002a. *Democracy for the Few.* 7th ed. New York: St. Martin's.

———. 2002b. *The Terrorism Trap: September 11 and Beyond.* San Francisco: City Lights.

Parrenas, Rhacel Salazar. 2001. *Servants of Globalization: Women, Migration and Domestic Work.* Stanford, Calif.: Stanford University Press.

Patnaik, Prabhat. 1999. "Capitalism in Asia at the End of the Millennium." *Monthly Review* 51, no. 3 (July–August).

Peet, Richard, ed. 1987. *International Capitalism and Industrial Restructuring.* Boston: Allen and Unwin.

Perlo, Victor. 1988. *Super Profits and Crises: Modern U.S. Capitalism.* New York: International.

Perrucci, Carolyn C., Robert Perrucci, Dena B. Targ, and Harry R. Targ. 1988. *Plant Closings: International Context and Social Costs.* New York: Aldine de Gruyter.

Peterson, R. Dean, Delores F. Wunder, and Harlan L. Mueller. 1999. *Social Problems: Globalization in the Twenty-first Century.* Upper Saddle River, N.J.: Prentice Hall.

Petras, James. 1978. *Critical Perspectives on Imperialism and Social Class in the Third World.* New York: Monthly Review.

———. 1981. *Class, State and Power in the Third World.* Montclair, N.J.: Allanheld, Osmun.

———. 1982. "Dependency and World System Theory: A Critique and New Directions." In *Dependency and Marxism,* ed. Ronald Chilcote. Boulder, Colo.: Westview.

———. 1998. *The Left Strikes Back: Class Conflict in Latin America in the Age of Neoliberalism.* Boulder, Colo.: Westview.

———. 2002. "U.S. Offensive in Latin America: Coups, Retreats, and Radicalization." *Monthly Review* 54, no. 1 (May).

Petras, James, and Christian Bay. 1990. "The Changing Wealth of the U.S. Ruling Class." *Monthly Review* 42, no. 7 (December).

———. 1993. "Cultural Imperialism in the Late 20th Century." *Journal of Contemporary Asia* 23, no. 2.

Petras, James, and Morris Morley. 1997. *U.S. Hegemony under Siege: Class Politics and Development in Latin America.* London: Verso.

Petras, James, and Henry Veltmeyer. 2001. *Globalization Unmasked: Imperialism in the 21st Century.* London: Zed.

Phillips, Brian. 1998. *Global Production and Domestic Decay: Plant Closings in the U.S.* New York: Garland.

Piazza, James A. 2002. *Going Global: Unions and Globalization in the United States, Sweden, and Germany.* Boulder, Colo.: Rowman and Littlefield.

Picciotto, Sol. 1990. "The Internationalization of the State." *Review of Radical Political Economics* 22, no. 1.

Pollack, Mark A., and Gregory C. Shaffer, eds. 2001. *Transatlantic Governance in the Global Economy.* Boulder, Colo.: Rowman and Littlefield.

Prazniak, Roxann, and Arif Dirlik, eds. 2001. *Places and Politics in an Age of Globalization.* Boulder, Colo.: Rowman and Littlefield.

Rai, Shirin. 2001. *Gender and the Political Economy of Development: From Nationalism to Globalization.* Cambridge: Polity.

Rajaee, Farhang. 2000. *Globalization on Trial: The Human Condition and the Information Civilization.* West Hartford, Conn.: Kumarian.

Rall, Ted. 2001. "It's about Oil." *San Francisco Chronicle,* 2 November.

———. 2002. "The New Great Game: Oil Politics in Central Asia." In *September 11 and the U.S. War: Beyond the Curtain of Smoke,* ed. Roger Burbach and Ben Clarke. San Francisco: City Lights.

Rantanen, Terhi. 2002. *The Global and the National.* Boulder, Colo.: Rowman and Littlefield.

Rao, C. P., ed. 1998. *Globalization, Privatization and Free Market Economy.* Westport, Conn.: Quorum.

Rashid, Ahmed. 2002. *Taliban: Militant Islam, Oil and Fundamentalism in Central Asia.* Waterville, Maine: Thorndike.

Rasler, Karen, and William R. Thompson. 1994. *The Great Powers and Global Struggle, 1490–1990.* Lexington: University of Kentucky Press.

Reifer, Thomas E., ed. 2002. *Hegemony, Globalization and Anti-systemic Movements.* Westport, Conn.: Greenwood.

Rennstich, Joachim K. 2001. "The Future of Great Power Rivalries." In *New Theoretical Directions for the 21st Century World-System,* ed. Wilma Dunaway. New York: Greenwood.

Renton, Dave. 2002. *Marx on Globalization.* London: Lawrence and Wishart.

Roberts, J. Timmons, and Amy Hite. 1999. *From Modernization to Globalization.* Oxford: Blackwell.

Robinson, William I. 1996. *Promoting Polyarchy: Globalization, U.S. Intervention, and Hegemony.* New York: Cambridge University Press.

———. 1998. "Beyond Nation-State Paradigms: Globalization, Sociology, and the Challenge of Transnational Studies." *Sociological Forum* 13.

Rodney, Walter. 1972. *How Europe Underdeveloped Africa.* Dar es Salaam: Tanzania Publishing.

Rosen, Ellen Israel. 2002. *Making Sweatshops: The Globalization of the U.S. Apparel Industry.* Los Angeles: University of California Press.

Ross, A. 1997. *No Sweat: Fashion, Free Trade, and the Rights of Garment Workers.* London: Verso.

Ross, Robert J. S. 1995. "The Theory of Global Capitalism: State Theory and Variants of Capitalism on a World Scale." In *A New World Order? Global Transformations in the Late Twentieth Century,* ed. David Smith and József Böröcz. Westport, Conn.: Praeger.

Ross, Robert J. S., and Kent C. Trachte. 1990. *Global Capitalism: The New Leviathan.* Albany: SUNY Press.

Rothman, Robert A. 2002. *Inequality and Stratification: Race, Class, and Gender.* 4th ed. Upper Saddle River, N.J.: Prentice Hall.

Roxborough, Ian. 1979. *Theories of Underdevelopment.* Atlantic Highlands, N.J.: Humanities.

Rowbotham, Sheila, and Stephanie Linkogle, eds. 2001. *Women Resist Globalization.* London: Zed.

Roy, Arundhati. 2002. "War Is Peace." In *September 11 and the U.S. War,* ed. Roger Burbach and Ben Clarke. San Francisco: City Lights.

Roy, Ash Narain. 1999. *The Third World in the Age of Globalization.* London: Zed.

Saenz, Mario, ed. 2002. *Latin American Perspectives on Globalization.* Boulder, Colo.: Rowman and Littlefield.

Salt, James. 1989. "Sunbelt Capital and Conservative Political Realignment in the 1970s and 1980s." *Critical Sociology* 16, nos. 2–3 (Summer–Fall).

Sau, Ranjit. 1992. "The Development of Monopoly Capital in India." In *Class, State, and Development in India,* ed. Berch Berberoglu. Delhi: Sage.

Saul, John S., and Colin Leys. 1999. *Monthly Review* 51, no. 3 (July–August).

Schaeffer, Robert K. 2003. *Understanding Globalization: The Social Consequences of Political, Economic, and Environmental Change.* 2nd ed. Boulder, Colo.: Rowman and Littlefield.

Scholte, Jan Aart. 2000. *Globalization: A Critical Introduction.* New York: Palgrave Macmillan.

Sen, Anupam. 1982. *The State, Industrialization, and Class Formations in India.* London: Routledge and Kegan Paul.

Servan-Schreiber, J. J. 1968. *The American Challenge.* New York: Atheneum.

Shepard, Benjamin, and Ronald Hayduk, eds. 2002. *From ACT UP to the WTO: Urban Protest and Community Building in the Era of Globalization.* London: Verso.

Sherman, Howard. 1976. *Stagflation.* New York: Harper and Row.

———. 1987. *Foundations of Radical Political Economy.* New York: Sharpe.

Siebert, Horst. 2000. *Globalization and Labor.* Kiel, Germany: Kiel Institute of World Economics.

Simon, Rick. 2000. "Class Struggle and Revolution in Eastern Europe: The Case of Poland." In *Marxism, the Millennium, and Beyond,* ed. Mark Cowling and Paul Reynolds. New York: Palgrave Macmillan.

Siochru, Sean O., and W. Bruce Girard with Amy Mahan. 2002. *Global Media Governance.* Boulder, Colo.: Rowman and Littlefield.

Sklair, Leslie. 1989. *Assembly for Development: The Maquila Industry in Mexico and the United States.* Boston: Unwin Hyman.

——. 1991. *Sociology of the Global System.* Baltimore, Md.: Johns Hopkins University Press.

——. 2001. *The Transnational Capitalist Class.* Malden, Mass.: Blackwell.

——. 2002. *Globalization: Capitalism and Its Alternatives.* New York: Oxford University Press.

Slaughter, Jane. 1990. "Is the Labor Movement Reaching a Turning Point?" *Labor Notes,* no. 130 (January).

Smith, Jackie G., and Hank Johnston, eds. 2002. *Globalization and Resistance: Transnational Dimensions of Social Movements.* New York: Routledge.

Smith, Joan. 1981. *Social Issues and the Social Order: The Contradictions of Capitalism.* Cambridge, Mass.: Winthrop.

Smith, Sheila. 1983. "Class Analysis versus World System: Critique of Samir Amin's Topology of Underdevelopment." In *Neo-Marxist Theories of Development,* ed. Peter Limqueco and Bruce McFarlane. New York: St. Martin's.

Stalker, Peter. 2000. *Workers without Frontiers: The Impact of Globalization on International Migration.* Boulder, Colo.: Rienner.

Starr, Amory. 2001. *Naming the Enemy: Anti-corporate Movements Confront Globalization.* London: Zed.

Stepan, Alfred. 1978. *The State and Society.* Princeton, N.J.: Princeton University Press.

Steven, Rob. 1994. "New World Order: A New Imperialism." *Journal of Contemporary Asia* 24, no. 3.

Stiglitz, Joseph E. 2002. *Globalization and Its Discontents.* New York: Norton.

Sugihara, Kaoru. 1993. "Japan, the Middle East and the World Economy." In *Japan in the Contemporary Middle East,* ed. K. Sugihara and J. A. Allan. London: Routledge.

Suter, Keith. 2000. *In Defense of Globalization.* Sydney: New South Wales University Press.

——. 2002. *Global Order and Global Disorder: Globalization and the Nation-State.* Westport, Conn.: Praeger.

Sweezy, Paul M., and Harry Magdoff. 1972. *The Dynamics of U.S. Capitalism.* New York: Monthly Review.

——. 1988. "The Stock Market Crash and Its Aftermath." *Monthly Review* 39, no. 10 (March).

Szymanski, Albert. 1974. "Marxist Theory and International Capital Flows." *Review of Radical Political Economics* 6, no. 3 (Fall).

——. 1978. *The Capitalist State and the Politics of Class.* Cambridge, Mass.: Winthrop.

——. 1981. *The Logic of Imperialism.* New York: Praeger.

Tabb, William K. 1997. "Globalization Is *An* Issue, the Power of Capital Is *the* Issue." *Monthly Review* 49, no. 2 (June).

——. 2001. *The Amoral Elephant: Globalization and the Struggle for Social Justice in the Twenty-first Century.* New York: Monthly Review.

Tamarov, Vladislav. 2001. *Afghanistan: A Russian Soldier's Story.* 2nd ed. Berkeley, Calif.: Ten Speed.

Tanzer, Michael. 1974. *The Energy Crisis: World Struggle for Power and Wealth.* New York: Monthly Review.

———. 1991. "Oil and the Gulf Crisis." *Monthly Review* 42, no. 11.

Teeple, Gary. 1995. *Globalization and the Decline of Social Reform.* Atlantic Highlands, N.J.: Humanity.

Tharamangalam, Joseph. 1992. "The Communist Movement and the Theory and Practice of Peasant Mobilization in South India." In *Class, State, and Development in India,* ed. Berch Berberoglu. Delhi: Sage.

Thomas, Janet. 2000. *The Battle in Seattle: The Story behind the WTO Demonstrations.* Golden, Colo.: Fulcrum.

Thompson, William R. 2000. *The Emergence of the Global Political Economy.* New York: Routledge.

Tigar, Michael E. 2001. "Terrorism and Human Rights." *Monthly Review* 53, no. 6 (November).

Tonelson, Alan. 2000. *The Race to the Bottom: Why a Worldwide Worker Surplus and Uncontrolled Free Trade are Sinking American Living Standards.* Boulder, Colo.: Westview.

Union for Radical Political Economics. 1978. *U.S. Capitalism in Crisis.* New York: Union for Radical Political Economics.

U.S. Bureau of the Census. Various Years. *Statistical Abstract of the United States.* Washington, D.C.: U.S. Government Printing Office.

U.S. Council of Economic Advisers. Various Years. *Economic Report of the President.* Washington, D.C.: U.S. Government Printing Office.

U.S. Department of Commerce. Various Issues. *Survey of Current Business.* Washington, D.C.: U.S. Government Printing Office.

U.S. Department of Labor, Bureau of Labor Statistics. 2003. "Employment Situation." News (January 10), at www.bls.gov/news.release/empsit.toc.htm (accessed February 14, 2003).

U.S. Office of Management and Budget. Various Years. *Budget of the United States Government.* Washington, D.C.: U.S. Government Printing Office.

Useem, Michael. 1989. "Revolt of the Corporate Owners and the Demobilization of Business Political Action." *Critical Sociology* 16, nos. 2–3 (Summer–Fall).

Valvano, Vince. 1988. "No Longer #1? Assessing U.S. Economic Decline." *Dollars and Sense,* no. 142 (December).

Van der Pijl, Kees. 1998. *Transnational Classes and International Relations.* New York: Routledge.

Vayrynen, Raimo, ed. 1999. *Globalization and Global Governance.* Boulder, Colo.: Rowman and Littlefield.

Vellinga, Menno, ed. 1999. *Dialectics of Globalization: Regional Responses to World Economic Processes: Asia, Europe, and Latin America in Comparative Perspective.* Boulder, Colo.: Westview.

Veltmeyer, Henry. 1999. "Labor and the World Economy." *Canadian Journal of Development Studies* 20 (Special Issue).

Vietor, Richard H. K., and Robert E. Kennedy. 2001. *Globalization and Growth: Cases in National Economics.* Fort Worth, Tex.: Harcourt.

Wagner, Helmut, ed. 2000. *Globalization and Unemployment.* New York: Springer.

Wallach, Lori, and Michelle Sforza. 1999. *Whose Trade Organization?: Corporate Globalization and the Erosion of Democracy.* Washington, D.C.: Public Citizen.

———. 2000. *The WTO: Five Years of Reasons to Resist Corporate Globalization.* New York: Seven Stories.

Wallerstein, Immanuel. 1974a. *The Modern World-System.* Vol. 1. New York: Academic.

———. 1974b. "The Rise and Future Demise of the World Capitalist System." *Comparative Studies in Society and History* 16, no. 4 (September).

———. 1979. *The Capitalist World-Economy.* Cambridge: Cambridge University Press.

———. 1980. *The Modern World-System.* Vol. 2. New York: Academic.

———. 1989. *The Modern World-System.* Vol. 3. New York: Academic.

———. 2002a. "The Eagle Has Crash Landed." *Foreign Policy* (July–August).

———. 2002b. "The United States in Decline?" In *Hegemony, Globalization, and Antisystemic Movements,* ed. Thomas E. Reifer. Westport, Conn.: Greenwood.

Warren, Bill. 1973. "Imperialism and Capitalist Industrialization." *New Left Review* 81 (September–October).

———. 1980. *Imperialism, Pioneer of Capitalism.* New York: Verso.

Waterman, Peter. 1998. *Globalization, Social Movements and the New Internationalisms.* London: Mansell.

Waters, Malcolm. 1995. *Globalization: The Reader.* New York: Routledge.

Weber, Steven, ed. 2001. *Globalization and the European Political Economy.* New York: Columbia University Press.

Webber, Michael John. 1996. *The Golden Age Illusion: Rethinking Postwar Capitalism.* New York: Guilford.

Weeks, John. 1981. *Capital and Exploitation.* Princeton, N.J.: Princeton University Press.

Went, Robert. 2000. *Globalization: Neoliberal Challenge, Radical Responses.* Trans. Peter Drucker. London: Pluto.

Werker, Scott. 1985. "Beyond the Dependency Paradigm." *Journal of Contemporary Asia* 15, no. 1.

Wynn, Sam. 1982. "The Taiwanese 'Economic Miracle.'" *Monthly Review* 33, no. 11 (April).

Yang, Xiaohua. 1995. *Globalization of the Automobile Industry: The United States, Japan, and the People's Republic of China.* Westport, Conn.: Praeger.

Yannopoulos, Dimitris. 2002. "Checkerboard of Oil, Minefields." In *September 11 and the U.S. War: Beyond the Curtain of Smoke,* ed. Roger Burbach and Ben Clarke. San Francisco: City Lights.

Yuen, Eddie, George Katsiaficas, and Daniel Burton Rose, eds. 2002. *The Battle of Seattle: The New Challenge to Capitalist Globalization.* New York: Soft Skull.

Zloch-Christy, Iliana, ed. 1998. *Eastern Europe and the World Economy: Challenges of Transition and Globalization.* Cheltenham, UK: Edward Elgar.

Zupnick, Elliot. 1999. *Visions and Revisions: The United States in the Global Economy.* Boulder, Colo.: Westview.

Index

161

About the Author

Berch Berberoglu is Foundation Professor of Sociology and the director of graduate studies in the department of sociology at the University of Nevada, Reno. He received his doctorate from the University of Oregon in 1977. He has been teaching and conducting research at the University of Nevada, Reno, for the past twenty-five years. Dr. Berberoglu has written and edited twenty books and many articles. His most recent books include *Political Sociology: A Comparative/Historical Approach* (2001) and *Labor and Capital in the Age of Globalization: The Labor Process and the Changing Nature of Work in the Global Economy* (2002). His areas of specialization include political economy, class analysis, development, and comparative-historical sociology. Dr. Berberoglu is currently working on *Class, State and Nation: Nationalism and Ethnic Conflict in the Age of Globalization,* which will be published in 2004.